A SHORT GUIDE TO
CONTRACT RISK

SHORT GUIDES TO RISK SERIES

Risk is a far more complex and demanding issue than it was ten years ago. Risk managers may have expertise in the general aspects of risk management and in the specifics that relate directly to their business, but they are much less likely to understand other more specialist risks. Equally, Company Directors may find themselves falling down in their duty to manage risk because they don't have enough knowledge to be able to talk to their risk team in a sensible way.

The short guides to risk are not going to make either of these groups experts in the subject but will give them plenty to get started and in a format and an extent (circa 150 pages) that is readily digested.

Titles in the series will include:

- Climate Risk
- Compliance Risk
- Employee Risk
- Environmental Risk
- Fraud Risk
- Information Risk
- Intellectual Property Risk
- Kidnap and Ransom Risk
- Operational Risk
- Purchasing Risk
- Reputation Risk
- Strategic Risk
- Supply Chain Risk
- Tax Risk
- Terrorism Risk

Visit www.gowerpublishing.com/shortguidestorisk for details of the latest titles, sample chapters and help on requesting a standing order.

A Short Guide to Contract Risk

Helena Haapio
Lexpert Ltd

George J. Siedel
University of Michigan

GOWER

Published by
Gower Publishing Limited
Wey Court East
Union Road
Farnham
Surrey GU9 7PT
England

Gower Publishing Company
110 Cherry Street
Suite 3-1
Burlington, VT 05401-3818
USA

www.gowerpublishing.com

British Library Cataloguing in Publication Data
Haapio, Helena.
  A short guide to contract risk. -- (Short guides to
  business risk series)
  1. Contracts. 2. Risk management.
  I. Title II. Series III. Siedel, George J.
  658.4'01-dc23

  ISBN: 978-1-4094-4886-0 (pbk)
  ISBN: 978-1-4094-4887-7 (ebk – PDF)
  ISBN: 978-1-4094-7365-7 (ebk – ePUB)

The Library of Congress has cataloged the printed edition as follows:
Haapio, Helena.
  A short guide to contract risk / by Helena Haapio and George J. Siedel.
    p. cm. -- (Short guides to business risk)
  Includes bibliographical references and index.
  ISBN 978-1-4094-4886-0 (pbk) -- ISBN 978-1-4094-4887-7 (ebook) -- ISBN 978-1-4094-7365-7 (epub) 1. Contracts--United States. 2. Risk management--United States. I. Siedel, George J. II. Title.
  KF801.H23 2013
  346.7302'2--dc23

                                                                    2012037710

MIX
Paper from
responsible sources
FSC
www.fsc.org   FSC® C018575

Printed and bound in Great Britain
by MPG PRINTGROUP

Contents

List of Figures

List of Tables

About the Authors

 **Helena Haapio** works as International Contract Counsel for Lexpert Ltd (www. lexpert.com), based in Helsinki, Finland. She helps her corporate clients use contracts and the law proactively to achieve better business results, balance risk with reward, and prevent legal trouble.

After completing legal studies at the University of Turku, Finland, and Cambridge University, England, Helena served for several years as in-house Legal Counsel in Finland, Norway, Sweden and the United States. Her responsibilities included drafting and negotiating contracts for complex international projects. She also arranged in-house training in related fields and was nominated Export Educator of the Year by the Finnish Institute for International Trade. She has designed and conducted corporate in-house and public training workshops on contract literacy, contractual risk management, and safe sales around the world.

Helena's current research focuses on proactive contracting, user-centered contract design, and visualization as means to enhance companies' ease of doing business and to simplify contracting processes and documents. She is the co-author of *Proactive Law for Managers—a Hidden Source of Competitive*

Advantage (Gower, 2011) and author and editor of many other publications. Helena is a member of the International Association for Contract and Commercial Management (IACCM, www.iaccm.com) Advisory Council and the founder and coordinator of IACCM Finland. She is actively involved in the development of the Nordic School of Proactive Law (www. proactivelaw.org) and of the ProActive ThinkTank (www. proactivethinktank.com). She also acts as arbitrator in cross-border contract disputes.

Helena can be contacted by email at Helena.Haapio@lexpert. com.

 **George J. Siedel** is Williamson Family Professor of Business Administration and Thurnau Professor of Business Law at the Ross School of Business, University of Michigan. He has served as Visiting Professor of Business Law at Stanford University, Visiting Professor of Business Administration at Harvard University, and Parsons Fellow at the University of Sydney.

His research interests relate to international business law, negotiation, and dispute resolution. Recent publications include the use of law to gain competitive advantage. George's work in progress focuses on the impact of litigation on large corporations, and the use of electronic communications in litigation. He has been admitted to practice before the United States Supreme Court and in Michigan, Ohio, and Florida. After completing graduate legal studies at the University of Michigan and Cambridge University, George worked as an attorney in a professional corporation. He has also served on several boards of directors and as Associate Dean for Executive Education at the Ross School of Business.

The author of numerous books and articles, George's research awards include the Faculty Recognition Award from the University of Michigan and the Hoeber Award from the Academy of Legal Studies in Business. The Center for International Business Education and Research selected a case he authored for its annual International Case Writing Award. He has been elected a Visiting Fellow at Cambridge University's Wolfson College and a Life Fellow of the Michigan State Bar Foundation. As a Fulbright Scholar, George held a Distinguished Chair in the Humanities and Social Sciences.

George can be contacted by email at gsiedel@umich.edu.

Acknowledgments

The authors want to acknowledge the contributions of Leila Hamhoum, Executive Assistant, Lexpert Ltd, to the successful completion of this book. The authors thank Martin West for recognizing the potential for the title as part of the Short Guide series and encouraging us to publish this book. Martin is Commissioning Editor for Gower Applied Research, which publishes books that emphasize the practical benefits to business that can arise from the intersection between theory and practice. Thanks also to the entire Gower team for their support.

We owe a special debt of gratitude to business, project, and risk managers and contracts and legal professionals with whom we have worked in Asia, Europe, the United States and South America. We are also indebted to the International Association for Contract and Commercial Management (IACCM) and Tim Cummins, whose surveys and ideas are mentioned a number of times throughout the text. And finally we thank the attendees at the corporate in-house and public workshops we have conducted in various parts of the world. Their enthusiasm has encouraged us to develop the framework of our earlier Gower title *Proactive Law for Managers* further and apply it to managing contract risks and opportunities for business success and problem prevention.

Helena Haapio and George J. Siedel
March 2013

Foreword

Risk is an ever-present feature of business operations, and its mastery is a source of potential profit and competitive advantage.

Contracts are a critical tool in the management of risk. However, the benefits of good contracting are frequently lost because there is a tendency by those who craft and negotiate them to focus on risk allocation or avoidance. This can often stifle opportunities and create a rigidity that threatens success.

In today's volatile business environment, uncertainty and change are inevitable. High-performing organizations are reassessing the role and purpose of contracts. They are taking steps to ensure they support sustainable relationships with terms and governance principles that encourage anticipation and collaboration in the management of risks. The focus is changing, with contracts increasingly measured by their success in delivering positive outcomes.

This book is a timely reminder to all business managers that they must equip themselves with the right tools to manage the inevitable risks that threaten their external relationships. Perhaps most importantly, it offers practical insights that enable our focus to shift from risk consequence to risk prevention—and will cause readers to view their contracts in a new and positive light, as true business assets.

Tim Cummins
Executive Director
International Association for Contract and Commercial Management (IACCM)

Reviews for
A Short Guide to Contract Risk

Contracts serve two primary functions—risk allocation and planning. Unfortunately, contracts as written in practice fail to perform either function very well. A Short Guide to Contract Risk does a wonderful job of showing these shortcomings and providing a user-friendly blueprint to shift the focus of contracts from risk allocation to risk prevention; from law-centered to performance-centered; and from breach-centered to dispute avoidance. This little book possesses a great deal of practical wisdom for the contracts scholar, legal practitioner, and business manager.

Professor Larry A. DiMatteo, Warrington College of Business Administration, University of Florida, USA

If you are looking for a concise, foundational primer on contract risk, you should read this book! I highly recommend it to anyone who has customer or vendor facing responsibility, or could in any way influence the negotiation or contract formation process. Although it does a nice job of addressing the core concept of risk inherent in business deals, it touches on far much more.

Timothy S. McCarthy, Director, Contracting and Negotiations, Rockwell Automation

I have welcomed their previous title Proactive Law for Managers *and now I am professionally very happy with the new book this successful duo has been able to compose. What I like most is the instrumental, proactive approach to business legal matters; in their own words: 'Contracts are not made for the legal department or future litigation; they are made for business, in order to reach business objectives' (introductory chapter). It is this managerial way of handling the law that is so needed in practice and yet so seldom seen in literature.*

Professor Antoni Brack, Twente
University, The Netherlands

Helena Haapio and George Siedel's book takes a fresh view on contracts. It is not just another book on contract law, but an easy to read, practically oriented guide on how to use contracts as a management rather than a legal tool. It provides innovative methods, examples and recommendations on how to manage contractual risk, prevent legal disputes, and effectively use contracts for business success. Insofar it skillfully bridges the gap between contract law and management, and I highly recommend it for both audiences.

Gerlinde Berger-Walliser, School of Business,
University of Connecticut, USA

The wide supply networks in different jurisdictions require new contract skills supporting the businesses targets and protecting the parties from excessive and surprising liabilities. The authors lift these skills directly to where they belong: in the companies' management and core processes. Contract management and clear responsibilities are an advantage for our customers in obtaining global liability insurance cover.

Matti Sjögren, Casualty Risk Management Specialist, If P&C Insurance Company Ltd., Industrial Risk Management

Projects and project business is characterized by complex transactions and uncertainty. Contract and well managed contracting process is an important tool for both managing risk and ensuring that project will deliver expected outcomes. Traditionally these two aspects have been dealt separately, lawyers focusing on risk avoidance and business people focusing on project business outcomes. Using proactive approach for contracting, the authors have done an excellent job in integrating these two views. The book provides practical tools and insight for business managers, project managers and lawyers how to improve contract and contracting process.

Professor Jaakko Kujala, University of Oulu, Finland

(1) Introduction

WHY THIS BOOK AND THIS TOPIC?

In today's business environment, contracts are everywhere. Contracts govern companies' deals and relationships with their suppliers and customers. They impact future rights, cash flows, costs, earnings, and risks. A company's contract portfolio may be subject to greater losses than anyone realizes. Still the greatest risk in business is not taking any risks. Contracts should support sound risk-taking and help balance risk with reward. This book is designed to help business, project and risk managers, as well as contracts and legal professionals, find and achieve the right balance.

These managers and professionals find themselves preparing or reviewing contracts, requests for proposals and quotations. Whether involved in sales, procurement or projects, many handle contractual data and documents on a daily basis, but very few have received training in the area. Many lack the confidence that comes with mastering the topic. Lawyers are not trained in *contracts* either—they are trained in *contract law*. Apart from contract law, success with contracts and contract risk requires knowledge and skills in many other aspects: technical, financial, operational, and so on.

If contracts fail, a lot is at stake. In addition to potential financial loss, goodwill and reputation may be at risk. Contract disputes are expensive and consume time and resources that should be used for productive work. Yet contract failure and disputes are not inevitable: using the *proactive approach* emphasized in this book, problems can be prevented and the likelihood of successful business relationships can be increased. This book offers knowledge, skills and tools that can help in this venture. At the same time, the book seeks to enhance collaboration and communication between business, project, and risk managers on one side and contracts and legal professionals on the other, across functions and disciplines.

The foundation of identifying and managing contract risk is what we call *contract literacy*: a set of skills relevant for all who deal with contracts in their everyday business environment, ranging from general managers and CEOs to sales, procurement and project professionals and from risk managers to contracts and legal professionals. Equipped with the concepts in this book, companies can start to see contracts differently and to use them for business success, problem prevention, and risk mitigation. This book focuses on contract risk and contract opportunities, suggesting ways in which companies can manage both.

This book is not targeted toward any specific country or industry. Its core content and examples are chosen so that they are applicable to contracting within and across borders anywhere. While the book uses examples involving companies, its core contents are useful for public organizations as well. Our focus, however, is on business-to-business dealings, where the parties can "make their own law" through their contract, which also includes the freedom to choose the law that applies. The book focuses on general problems and general solutions and is not meant to supply direction on how to handle legal issues, or to provide or replace legal or other expert advice. Appropriate legal or other professional advice should always be obtained and relied upon before taking or omitting to take action in respect of any specific problem.

While the authors of this book are lawyers and we discuss a number of legal aspects related to contracts, we do not see contracts merely as legal tools. Contracts are not made for the legal department or future litigation; they are made for business, in order to reach business objectives. Among these objectives, winning in litigation hardly ever takes top priority. So we seek to take a balanced, down-to-earth, managerial–legal approach. Our goal is to enable shared understanding that leads to legally sound contracts, contracts that can be used as managerial tools for well thought-out, realistic risk allocation in business deals and relationships and that are implemented successfully in a way that meets the parties' expectations.

This book is designed to help companies use their contracts and contracting processes proactively to achieve their business plans and to think through potential contingencies that may affect the outcomes of their projects, deals and relationships. The book demonstrates the increasing importance of contracts and the risks and opportunities they pose, illustrates the potential impact of exposure to contract risk, and outlines the key elements of effective risk management, along with ways to negotiate successful, risk-aware contracts.

WHO "OWNS" CONTRACT RISKS?

Today's companies possess a wide range of contract-related and risk management-oriented skills and capabilities, yet these are often fragmented. It is not easy to transform the skills and knowledge of individuals to organization-level competence. Despite the obvious benefits of managing contract risk in a systematic way, challenges remain for someone wishing to change the ways a company sees and treats contracts and risk. One of the major challenges is the current "dual ownership" of contracting processes and documents. While *contracting* (as part of selling, purchasing, alliancing, networking, and so on) is a business process and business management is in charge of its outcomes, *contracts* often seem to fall into the sole domain of lawyers.

Who, then, is in charge of the contracts a company makes— or of the processes through which contracts are made, implemented and managed? Who is in charge of managing the risks related to them? Who is their "owner?" Is it wise when, first, the sales or account manager is in charge, then during negotiations the contracts or legal professionals take over, and after contract signing the project manager or the implementation team (along with the production or operations manager and eventually field or support services) take charge? When this happens, the right hand does not always know what the left hand is doing. Roles and responsibilities relating to obligations, tasks, costs, implementation, and risk may remain unclear and may cause confusion inside the company and among its customers, suppliers, and subcontractors. Buy-side contracts and warranties may not support sell-side contracts and warranties, and supply contracts may not be coordinated with insurance. Individual's responsibilities and the extent of their authority are not always completely clear.

As the number of people who work with contracts grows, questions about how the contract portfolio is administered and used and how its risks are managed need to be addressed. If the company operates multiple facilities in different locations and countries and its business units are independent, the difficulties increase. The company is not always aware of the contracts made in the different business units and whether the units' contract processes and documents are up to date. Information about aggregate liabilities or risks might not be available quickly. Purchasing power is hard to leverage if the units do not know that they are using common suppliers or the value of their total purchases. On the sell-side, payment terms, warranty periods, liabilities and other terms may vary significantly between the different business units and also between the different product and service groups within one unit.

On the business operations' level, somebody must ensure that the interests of the different units, functions and professionals are aligned. Contracts must be easy to use and effective, and they must be legally valid. Risks must be reasonable in relation to the anticipated benefits, and the costs of contracting must not become excessive. Operations and resources need to be managed, and processes need to be repeatable. Healthy bureaucracy is needed—but at the same time, creativity, innovativeness, and flexibility are also important. The strengths of different professional groups must be merged and the various roles and responsibilities must be coordinated. While a matrix can help define the areas of responsibility of each group or function, somebody must be in charge of integrating the different areas.

Who then is this "somebody" who is in charge of integrating the various skill sets, actions, documents and interests related to contracts, risks, and their management? The answer varies from one organization and from one project to another. The sales, procurement, project, risk or contract manager can be in charge of a major part of the whole. However, business leaders and executives are ultimately responsible for business results. So ultimately the responsibility for business contracts and for organizing the management of contract risks will normally fall on the shoulders of business leaders and executives. In any case, their attitude towards contracts determines how the opportunities offered by contracts are used—or whether they are used at all.

Executive management can delegate the responsibility for contracts and for managing the related risk, as long as this is visible in the job description of the person(s) to whom it is delegated. Responsibility is connected to the question of authority and a common understanding is needed regarding both. What matters most is clarity for everybody involved.

A FRESH PERSPECTIVE: A PROACTIVE APPROACH

Savvy managers no longer look at contracting processes and documents reactively, but use them *proactively* to reach their business objectives. The *proactive approach* adopted in this book has two dimensions, both of which emphasize forward-looking action: a *preventive* dimension, seeking to prevent problems and disputes, and a *promotive* dimension, seeking to secure the respective actors' success in reaching their goals. In the context of this book, this means using contracting processes and documents proactively to (1) decrease the possibility and impact of failure and negative events; (2) increase the possibility and impact of business success and positive events; and (3) enable sound risk-taking, which includes balancing risk with reward. Success requires attention to both risks and opportunities, along with their causes, likelihood, and effects.

Contracts are known for being effective risk-allocation tools. However, legal and business priorities may differ. While this book discusses ways in which contracts can be used to allocate risk, we do not stop there. Success requires *contract literacy* of the organization and its supply chain—in fact, the entire extended enterprise. Armed with this contract literacy, those involved in the contracting process can move beyond allocating risk to managing risk. Moreover, they can use their contracting processes and documents to realize business benefits and manage opportunities for value creation.

To reach their business objectives, companies seldom need legally "perfect" contracts; they need usable, practical contracts that achieve desired business goals and reasonable risk allocation at an acceptable cost. Contracts do not make things happen—*people* do. People need to know what their contracts require them to do, where, and when. Today's complex contracts are seldom easy for their users in the field, mostly non-lawyers, to understand and to implement. If contract language and complexity overload readers' cognitive abilities, contract implementation will fail. Such contracts—even if they are legally "perfect"—are far from good, operationally efficient contracts and fall short of their ultimate purpose. This is where a fresh perspective represented by what we call *lean contracting* and *contract visualization* enters the picture. Along with the proactive approach, this fresh perspective helps move from a "contracts are *legal* tools" attitude toward seeing contracts as *managerial* tools. At the same time, these approaches seek to change the view of contracts as *risk allocation* tools, made to win in court and needed only when things go wrong, to seeing contracts as value-adding devices and as enablers of business success that help the parties *manage risk together*. These aspects are presented in Figure 1.1.

Figure 1.1   A fresh perspective

For companies, *the contract* itself is not the goal; *successful implementation* is. So we take the view that the core of contract design should be securing the *performance* and *business benefits* the parties expect, not just a legal contract. Success in managing contract risks and opportunities often requires changing the ways corporate contracting works: from pre-contract to negotiation and signing and then to post-contract stages. This, in turn, requires the involvement of both business management and the legal department. Both need to see the need for change and must be willing and able to change their current ways of working.

HOW THIS BOOK IS ORGANIZED

In Chapter 1, we have provided a brief introduction to the topic and have explained the sometimes challenging managerial–legal "dual ownership" of contracting processes and documents. We have also briefly introduced our approach to contracts, risks and opportunities: the *proactive approach*.

In Chapter 2, we present the big picture by asking why companies make contracts. After defining the core concepts used in this book, such as "contract," "risk," and "contract risk," we discuss the business and legal objectives at risk and the *promotive, preventive, and balancing power* of contracts. We then introduce what we consider the foundation of identifying and managing contract risk: *contract literacy.*

Chapter 3 provides an overview of the sources of contract risk. It illustrates how contract wording or legal issues, while they are important when resolving legal disputes, are not the primary sources of contract risk. After introducing what we consider to be the true risk sources, we discuss current contract practices and how these must change.

Chapter 4 focuses on risks in negotiating the business contract, such as legal risks that arise in contract formation, the risk that negotiators will use negotiating strategies that cause them to overlook opportunities to create value that will benefit both sides, and the risks associated with a deal-maker mindset. The chapter also introduces *lean contracting* as a method that enables the development of contracts that are management as well as legal tools.

In Chapter 5, we cover risks inherent in a contract itself. We address performance concerns and legal concerns, along with the most frequent sources of claims and disputes. We discuss contract clauses and issues that are typically considered to be risky and how to respond to them through the use of exclusion and limitation clauses and other conventional contract risk allocation devices. While *contract literacy* recognizes the importance of being able to identify devices used to respond to risk, the chapter also illustrates how true risk management needs to go beyond them. Chapter 5 also illustrates, with examples, how what is *left out* of a contract—knowingly or unknowingly—can be at least as important as what is included.

Chapter 6 provides tools and techniques to secure systematic contract risk recognition and response. The chapter's introduction of the contract risk management process and the contract risk and opportunity management plan is followed with examples of how you can apply them. In addition to the more traditional tools, the chapter introduces *visualization* as a new approach to simpler contracting and enhanced risk and opportunity management. The lean and visual (IKEA) approach to contracts, risks, and their management illustrates how the parties can *manage risks jointly* and move from contractual *risk allocation* to true contractual *risk management*.

In conclusion, Chapter 7 provides a short summary of key actions that enable you to implement the practices described in this book and to make full use of your contracts to achieve your business objectives while recognizing and managing contract risks and opportunities.

② Contracts and Risk—the Big Picture

WHY DO COMPANIES MAKE CONTRACTS?

For traditional thinkers, contracts are legal tools. They are about promises that the law will enforce. Contracts create rights and responsibilities, and the law will provide remedies if contractual promises are broken. For the purposes of this book, such a view is too limited and too legalistic.

Experience and research prove the growing importance of contracts for today's extended and interconnected enterprise. Companies do not make contracts just for the legal department or future litigation; they make contracts to enable business to reach business objectives. Apart from being legal tools, contracts are management tools, not only in terms of risk but also in terms of opportunities for value creation, successful inter-firm collaboration, profitability, and competitive advantage.[1]

---

1   See, for example, Siedel, G. and Haapio, H. (2011) *Proactive Law for Managers: A Hidden Source of Competitive Advantage*. Farnham: Gower Publishing, and Argyres, N.S. and Mayer, K.J. (2007) Contract design as a firm capability. *Academy of Management Review*, 32(4), October, 1060–77.

Today's business takes place in an increasingly complex, global and networked environment where contracts play a key role. Major business decisions crystallize into a contract or agreement of some sort. Projects ranging from construction and equipment supply to IT acquisition and outsourcing all involve contracts, both on the sell-side and on the buy-side. Collaborative R&D, selling, procurement, finance, invoicing, change control, claims and many other fields operate within the framework of contracts.

In collaborative ventures and large projects with multiple suppliers and subcontractors, the interfaces among the various providers must be managed well. Required actions must be taken at the right time and in the right place by one's own organization and by the other parties. The required coordination, communication and control can be provided by contracts.

When used as managerial tools, contracts can help to coordinate and manage business, projects, and commitments; to create, allocate and protect value, whether tangible or intangible (such as intellectual property rights); to communicate crucial information inside and between organizations; to motivate; and to allocate decision and control rights. Contracts also enable companies to share, minimize and manage risk; to prevent problems; and to keep problems from developing into disputes. Where a dispute is unavoidable, contracts provide evidence of what has been agreed and an effective means to control and resolve the dispute. The main functions of contracts can be summarized as follows:[2]

---

2   Siedel and Haapio 2011, p. 118. Originally published in Haapio, H. and Haavisto, V. (2005) Sopimusosaaminen: tulevaisuuden kilpailutekijä ja strateginen voimavara. [Contracting capabilities: Emerging source of competitive advantage and a strategic resource]. *Yritystalous—Leader's Magazine*, 63(2), 7–15.

Contracts are tools for:

1. Managing business, projects and commitments
2. Creating, allocating and protecting value
3. Communication, coordination, motivation, and control
4. Sharing, minimizing and managing risk
5. Problem prevention, dispute avoidance and resolution

Good-quality contracts serve as *visible scripts* for parties working together.

One way to look at contracts is to see them as *visible scripts*—blueprints, roadmaps or sets of instructions—for collaboration. Contracting processes and documents can help make requirements, roles, and responsibilities—along with related risks—visible. In this way, contracts can serve as tools for articulating and aligning expectations and *planning* and *managing* business, projects and relationships. The chapters that follow will show how businesses can use their contracts to actively manage risk and the realization of benefits.

WHAT EXACTLY DO WE MEAN BY "CONTRACT" AND "CONTRACTING?"

When hearing the word "contract," most people have a tendency to think of formal, legal documents. Many tend to categorize contracts under "law" and think that contracts are best left for lawyers. Traditional project management literature seems to have a rather narrow and legalistic view of contracts also. For example, the Project Management Institute's (PMI) *Guide to the Project Management Body of Knowledge*, when discussing project procurement management, notes that a contract is "a legal relationship subject to remedy in the courts."[3] No wonder many business and project managers have chosen not to get involved and delegate contracts to lawyers. We take a different view: as war is too important to be left to the generals alone, contracts are too important to be left to the lawyers alone.

So what do we mean by contracts? The word "contract" has two basic meanings: (1) an agreement (a bargain, a deal) and (2) the document representing the agreement (or attempting to represent it—documents are often not complete embodiments of an agreement). Contracts can take many forms and they can be created in many different ways. They may be signed documents, engagement letters, or a chain of letters or electronic messages. Contracts may be formed, for instance, through an offer (bid, quotation) followed by a purchase order, or through a purchase order followed by an order confirmation. As we will see later in this book, the basic requirements of contracts are not the same throughout the world or in all contexts. In some cases, to be valid, contracts need to be in writing; in others, they do not. In some countries and contexts, the formation of a valid contract requires that each side provides something of value, *consideration*; in others, it does not.

Not all contracts are documents with the word "contract" on top; in fact, contracts are not always easy to recognize. Still it is important to note that in every sale and purchase of goods

---

3   *A Guide to the Project Management Body of Knowledge (PMBOK® Guide)* (2000) Newtown Square, PA: Project Management Institute (PMI), p. 156. The same can be found in the more recent 2004 and 2008 editions of the *Guide* (2004, p. 289; 2008, p. 333). In the glossary of the *Guide*, a contract is defined as a "mutually binding agreement that obligates the seller to provide the specified product or service or result and obligates the buyer to pay for it" (2000, p. 199; 2004, p. 355; 2008, p. 429).

or services and in every collaborative venture where two or more companies work together, a contract is present. It may be written or unwritten, formal or informal. Its terms may be stated, for instance, in a customized document or a standard form, and it may contain appendices such as technical specifications, work scope definitions, and Standard Terms and Conditions (STCs; "the small print"). Offers, purchase (or change) orders, confirmations, memoranda, letters of intent and the like, even email messages, can also change contracts. Their contractual aspects need to be recognized and properly addressed. In addition, contracts often contain important requirements for operational performance, milestones, invoices, reports, and notices that need to be captured and followed in daily business.

All of the above are relevant in the context of contracts and risk, and they need to be managed. Preparing, negotiating, and signing documents are important steps in the contracting process, but there is more. If contracts are forgotten in a drawer and not followed, businesses can open themselves to a multitude of risks and lose many of the benefits they have sought to secure.

In today's complex, multi-locational deals, contracting is rarely a craft activity conducted by an expert at a desk who produces a written document bearing the heading "contract." Today's contracting is a process in which a wide range of people, functions and technologies are involved: a collaborative venture that requires a knowledgeable and well-connected team. The vertical dashed line in the center of Figure 2.1 depicts the moment when a contract is made and signed, often understood to be "contracting" in the narrow meaning of the word.

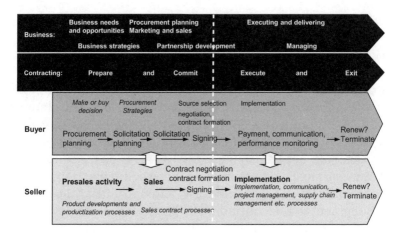

Figure 2.1   Contracting and business processes[4]

The term "contracting" is used here to refer not only to *preparing* and *making* but also to *managing* and *implementing* contracts (or, as is often the case, a portfolio of contracts). For our purposes, it is useful to break down the contracting process into phases: (1) planning, solicitation and bidding (pre-award); (2) negotiation and signing (award); and (3) implementation, performance and administration (post-award). Figure 2.1 shows how the business and contracting processes of suppliers and buyers are intertwined and emphasizes the significance of implementation as part of the contracting process.

---

4   *Contracting Capabilities in Industrial Life-Cycle and Service Business.* Research Report. A summarized version in English is available at http://www.uef.fi/oikeustieteet/ ccc. Reprinted with the permission of Professor Soili Nystén-Haarala, under whose leadership the multidisciplinary Corporate Contracting Capabilities research project was conducted in Finnish firms in 2006–2008.

WHAT EXACTLY DO WE MEAN BY "RISK?"

Risk means different things to different people. Both upside and downside can be included. David Hillson, known as the Risk Doctor, has simplified the definition of risk by calling risk "uncertainty that matters."[5] More complex definitions exist. For example, the international ISO Risk Management Standard (ISO 31000:2009) defines risk as *an effect of uncertainty on objectives*. This effect—a deviation from the expected—can be positive or negative. Uncertainty, again, is defined in the standard as "the state, even partial, of deficiency of information related to, understanding or knowledge of, an event, its consequence, or likelihood." A more basic definition would be to say that uncertainty means *lack of certainty*.

The 2008 edition of the US-based PMI *Guide to the Project Management Body of Knowledge*[6] *defines risk as an uncertain event or condition that, if it occurs, has a positive or negative effect on a project's objectives*. The Risk Management Standard of the major risk management organizations in the UK— the Institute of Risk Management (IRM), the Association of Insurance and Risk Managers (AIRMIC) and the National Forum for Risk Management in the Public Sector (ALARM)— defines risk slightly differently as *the combination of the probability of an event and its consequences*, stating that in all types of undertakings, there is the potential for events and consequences that constitute opportunities for benefit (upside) or threats to success (downside).[7]

5   See, for instance, Hillson, D. and Murray-Webster, R. (2007) *Understanding and Managing Risk Attitude*, 2nd edn. Farnham: Gower Publishing, p. 5, and briefings and articles available at http://www.risk-doctor.com.
6   *PMBOK® Guide* (2008) 4th edn. Newtown Square, PA: Project Management Institute (PMI).
7   *A Risk Management Standard* (2002) IRM, AIRMIC and ALARM, available at http://www.theirm.org/publications/documents/Risk_Management_Standard_030820.pdf.

In this book, the word "risk" is used for the downside: the possibility that something unpleasant or unwelcome will happen, leading to unfavorable outcomes. What the above definitions see as "upside risk," we call "opportunity." In this way, we distinguish between risk (or threat) and opportunity: we use the word risk (or threat) for uncertain events that could affect objectives adversely, while we use the word opportunity for uncertain events that could affect objectives beneficially.

CONTRACT RISK: UNCERTAINTY THREATENING THE ACHIEVEMENT OF OBJECTIVES

We are not aware of any standards attempting to define *contract risks*. Contract risks are sometimes seen as part of legal or liability risks and contractual risk management is seen as a subset of legal risk management.[8] The company may face liability if it breaches its contractual obligations. It may incur harmful consequences if it fails to implement its contracts, if its contracts are invalid, or if contract documentation is defective or lacking. False claims in contracts or related sales documentation may subject a company to liability for breach of contract, breach of warranty, fraud, or deceptive trade practices, and so on.

Contract risks can be caused by the other party—for example, its inability or unwillingness to pay or to otherwise fulfil its obligations. When a company operates in the middle of a supply chain, its sell-side and buy-side contracts may not support each other. When this happens, the contract chain

---

8   See, for example, Mahler, T. (2010) Legal risk management—developing and evaluating elements of a method for proactive legal analyses, with a particular focus on contracts. Doctoral thesis, Faculty of Law, Oslo: University of Oslo.

may break and result in a loss. If contracts are unclear, the probability of problems developing will grow. In some contexts, certain regulations such as consumer protection laws or competition laws may also add to contract risks.

While contract risks may lead to disputes and litigation, they extend beyond legal issues, such as damages and remedies for breach. If we define risk in terms of uncertainty related to reaching objectives or as a possible negative deviation from the expected, what, then, are the objectives that may be at risk in the context of contracts?

The answer will depend on the context—for example, whether we are discussing a company, a business unit, or a project—and on whom we ask. An entrepreneur might say that business results are at risk: contracts are made to accomplish business results. An accountant might say that cash flow and assets are at risk: contracts are made so that money, products and services can predictably change hands and reliable accounts can be kept on who owns what and who owes what to whom. A project manager might say that successful project outcomes are at risk: contracts are a way to set goals and monitor results in terms of time, money and quality. A lawyer might say that a company's entire financial future may be at risk: contracts are needed to clarify commitments, exclude undesirable and unknown liability, limit excessive risk exposure, and control and resolve disputes.

It is hard to disagree with any of these answers. They represent different functions of contracts and different professions' and individuals' varying views on what matters most. Contracts are tools to reach all of the above objectives—but they can only do so if they are properly designed and a balance is found between the different (and sometimes conflicting) objectives.

Contract risks may threaten business deals and relationships, reduce margins, and prevent the parties from achieving their objectives. They may cause unexpected costs or unintended liabilities. In this book, we use the words "contract risk" for risks that can lead to a negative deviation from the *expected outcomes of a contract*. These may be business outcomes, legal outcomes, or both. Contract risks are about uncertainty related to reaching objectives. They threaten the success of a contract and can lead to a negative deviation from what is expected.

Contract Risks

- threaten the success of a contract
- are about uncertainty related to reaching objectives
- can lead to a negative deviation from what is expected
- can impact business objectives, legal objectives, or both.

What is viewed as success also depends on whose view we represent. What appears as a source of contract risk to one party—for example, the buyer—may appear to be contract risk management (or risk allocation) to the other party, in this case the supplier. The views of the buy-side and sell-side differ, as do those of business and legal.

In this book, we see *reaching business objectives* as the ultimate goal of contracts. Viewed in this way, contracts become *business benefit realization tools*. The objectives and benefits depend on the business and the situation at hand and may relate, for instance, to profit, cash flow, completion of work, uninterrupted service delivery, or access to resources such as funding, information, or talent. In this context, *contract risk* is the possibility that the contract leads to a negative deviation from the expected business outcomes, such as when objectives are not achieved at all, on time, or to cost/budget, quality, or performance expectations.

Contract risk can also lead to a negative deviation from the expected legal outcomes. For instance, the contract or some of its terms that were expected to be valid may not be legally binding and enforceable. This may lead to one party abandoning the contract and the other being left with no performance or remedy. While freedom of contract is the basic principle governing contract law, there are limits to this freedom. There also might be requirements as to form and other requirements that sometimes vary from one legal system to another, and the parties do not want to be negatively surprised. One of the legal objectives of contracts is to create clarity about the binding force of contracts and their terms. Further, contracts should pass the tests of legal accuracy and clarity.

Often, the business and legal objectives of contracts are intertwined, and a negative deviation from one objective can lead to challenging the other. Negative surprises that have a commercial impact can lead to a dispute and invoke the legal dimensions of the contract. Parties who did not read the contract earlier will soon realize that even the small print may have a big impact. Different contracts and sources of contract law may provide different and unexpected results. Even the provisions related to the choice of law and settlement of disputes might have a major impact on the outcome of the dispute and whether the judgement or arbitral award can be enforced.

In addition to success and desirable outcomes that a business wants, there are outcomes that a business *does not want*—for instance, resources spent in excess of what is budgeted, revenue leakage, losses, delays, conflicts leading to disputes and litigation. These result in negative deviations from the expected outcomes. Whether one classifies them as contract risks, business risks, project risks, or legal risks is not important; the main point is that businesses should be aware of the opportunities offered by their contracts to manage these risks and to realize business benefits.

CONTRACT OPPORTUNITIES: FAVORABLE OUTCOMES, BENEFITS AND PREDICTABILITY

Despite its importance for business and entrepreneurs, contract opportunity is a surprisingly recent topic for practical and theoretical discussion. Corporate risk managers are in an established profession, opportunity managers are not. While contract risks and legal risks are frequently discussed, contract opportunities and legal opportunities are not.

Contract opportunities can be viewed in many different ways. One way is to see them as opportunities offered by contracts. This book will discuss these opportunities, including opportunities to use contracting processes and documents to remove uncertainty and provide predictability; to articulate, align, and clarify expectations; to coordinate and manage internal and external resources; and to manage and monitor quality, projects, and risks. *Contract opportunity* can also mean "upside risk" in the content of contracts: events that could affect contractual objectives beneficially, or the possibility that a contract will lead to a positive deviation from the expected outcomes. Again, these outcomes may be business outcomes or legal outcomes.

When used proactively, contracts can help *remove uncertainty* and *provide predictability*. This opportunity offered by contracts can be used to remove uncertainty related to performance and the parties' roles, rights, and duties. Or it can be used to remove uncertainty from the contract formation process by providing the parties with confidence that the legally binding commitment is clear. For lawyers, predictability is also about predicting the way in which a contract, intertwined with the applicable law, will be interpreted and applied if a legal dispute arises.

As noted earlier, reaching *business objectives* should be the ultimate goal of contracts. From a business point of view, exceeding those objectives is a good thing. From a legal point of view, things may look slightly different. In a legal assessment of contracts, *any* deviation—even one that a business person might normally welcome, such as early delivery or delivery of excess quantity, can be risky. Unless expressly provided for in the contract, a deviation can constitute a breach of contract— even when the likelihood of a loss and a claim are non-existent. For example, delivery of excess quantity can constitute a breach that might be used by a buyer looking for a reason to terminate the contract. In contract law, there are many categories of negative deviations and their consequences, while positive deviations are hardly ever touched upon. Even in other fields, extraordinary performance, exceeding expectations, and positive deviance are seldom discussed in the context of contracts.[9]

---

9   Exceptions include Cameron, K. and Lavine, M. (2006) *Making the Impossible Possible. Leading Extraordinary Performance. The Rocky Flats Story.* San Francisco: Berrett-Koehler Publishers. The book is about the contract for the cleaning up of the Rocky Flats nuclear weapons plant. Estimates projected that the cleaning up and closing of the facility would take 70 years and cost US\$36 billion. The project was completed 60 years ahead of schedule and US\$30 billion under budget.

Practitioners and researchers agree that the concept "opportunity" clearly refers to something favorable, something that will have a positive impact on objectives, yet they have different views as to its definition, causes, and effects. Two schools of thought exist: one suggesting that opportunities are *discovered* and another suggesting that opportunities are *created*. We take the view that it is equally important to create opportunities as it is to discover them. Contracts offer tools for both. As we will see later in this book, contracts offer opportunities for requirements management, quality management, and risk management. When a disturbance occurs, contracts can help bring the relationship back on track. Even contract risks may offer opportunities: a claim may bring opportunities for additional sales or new product development.

Whether the aim is to reach or to exceed contractual objectives, businesses should not let an overly legalistic view of contracts prevent them from recognizing and making use of contract opportunities. As already stated, perceptions and attitudes play a major role here. If the attitude is "contracts are just for lawyers," business managers will alienate themselves from the contracting process and thereby lose opportunities for favorable outcomes, benefits and predictability that contracts can offer.

THE PROMOTIVE, PREVENTIVE AND BALANCING POWER OF CONTRACTS

Contract risk can be caused or increased by a failure to appreciate the importance of good contracting or by an "any contract will work" attitude. After a contract risk has materialized and a loss has occurred, it might be too late to change your contractual rights and responsibilities. As stated by Louis M. Brown, "when you 'sign on the dotted line', you obligate yourself; before you sign, you have a freedom of choice not available later."[10] As noted in Chapter 1, the *proactive approach* adopted in this book builds on and enables using contracting processes and documents proactively to (1) decrease the possibility and impact of negative events; (2) increase the possibility and impact of positive events; and (3) enable sound risk taking, which includes balancing risk with reward. In the following discussion, we call these the (1) preventive; (2) promotive; and (3) balancing power of contracts.

Contracts may lead to unexpected losses or other negative outcomes, such as misunderstandings, delays, claims, or disputes. If contracts fail, business performance will suffer. A lot is at stake, including goodwill and reputation. Contract disputes are expensive, in terms of money, management, and staff time that could be used for productive work. However, using the *preventive power* of contracts, unnecessary causes of problems can be eliminated and their negative impact can be minimized. In addition, contracts can be designed to provide procedures for handling problem situations and resolution mechanisms if delays or disturbances occur or if a conflict arises.

The pyramid diagram in Figure 2.2—borrowed from preventive law, which in turn borrowed it from preventive medicine—prompts us to think along three basic domains of prevention: first, prevent the cause from arising; second, prevent the cause from doing harm; and third, if harm occurs, limit the damage. This way of thinking leads us to develop strategies and tools

---

10   Louis M. Brown, known as the Father of Preventive Law, in *How to Negotiate a Successful Contract* (1955) Englewood Cliffs, NJ: Prentice-Hall, Inc., p. vii.

to minimize friction and keep causes of risk and problems from arising (level one); to seek early intervention to prevent causes of risk from doing harm and problems from becoming disputes (level two); and to mitigate risk and resolve conflict to limit losses and expense (level three).

These measures are intertwined: as will be seen later in this book, contractual conflict prevention is not restricted to dispute resolution clauses alone. One of the most powerful ways to prevent and control disputes between contracting parties is to rationally allocate risks by assigning each potential risk to the party who is best able to manage, control or insure against the particular risk. Conversely, unrealistic shifting of risks to a party who is not equipped to handle the risk can increase costs, sow the seeds of disputes, create distrust and resentment, and establish adversarial relationships that can interfere with the success of the business enterprise.[11]

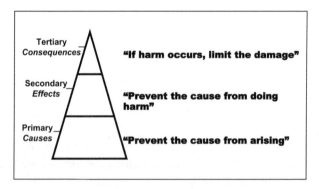

Figure 2.2   The three domains of prevention

11   See, for example, Groton, J.P. and Haapio, H. (2007) *From Reaction to Proactive Action: Dispute Prevention Processes in Business Agreements.* International Association for Contract and Commercial Management EMEA Academic Symposium, London, 9 October 2007, available at http://www.iaccm.com/loggedin/library/nonphp/Paper 7 – From Reaction to Proactive Action – Dispute Prevention Processes in Business Agreements.pdf.

Using the *promotive power* of contracts increases the likelihood and impact of business success and helps identify, create, and maximize opportunities. If the focus in contracting is on realizing business benefits and on success (rather than failure, which is currently often the case), the *promotive power* of contracts can be used to its full potential. The likelihood of successful outcomes and business benefits can be enhanced when contract preparation and negotiation do not take too long and when they focus on effective implementation. In this way, unnecessary friction and misunderstandings can be avoided, resulting in faster order intake, earlier performance and cash flow, better business relationships, and reputational goodwill. Optimally, these will lead to cost reductions, more benefits, and earlier benefits for both parties.

Apart from enabling the parties to reach their business objectives and prevent problems and disputes, contracts have one more capability that is important in the context of reaching business and legal objectives; using the *balancing power* of contracts, the parties can balance risk with reward. They can—and should—do so both in their own decision making and when considering the needs and interests of the other party. A supply contract, for example, should ensure that the supplied goods, services, or solutions will meet the buyer's requirements, while at the same time satisfying the supplier's needs and expectations relating to profitability and risk. In an ideal situation, the risks taken by the contracting parties are identified and reflected in the parties' roles and responsibilities as well as in the requirements, scope, price, schedule, and other terms. The balancing power of contracts is illustrated in Figure 2.3.

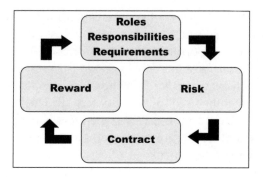

Figure 2.3   The balancing power of contracts

An ideal contract also balances the legal needs and business needs of the parties, including the need for predictability and flexibility. A contract should not limit the parties' ability to innovate in the future, nor should it involve *unidentified* requirements, responsibilities or remedies that reduce profits or other expected benefits or increase cost or risk. Here we are not talking about contract provisions that are accepted, with eyes wide open, as legitimate trade-offs. Rather, we are talking about unexpected, unfavorable terms that could have been avoided or mitigated by using thorough preparation, skillful negotiation, and the promotive, preventive, and balancing power of contracts.

As noted earlier, contracts seek to secure clarity and remove uncertainty as to business and legal objectives and how the parties plan to work together to reach those objectives. Contracts can help *provide predictability*. When the power of contracts is used at the early stages, the crafting of a contract becomes an important initial step in articulating the business plan, in thinking through potential contingencies that may affect it, and in achieving business objectives. Viewed in this way, contracts can help align expectations, encourage innovation, improve supply chain performance, provide adequate protection, and balance risks against rewards and benefits.

CONTRACT LITERACY: THE FOUNDATION FOR IDENTIFYING AND MANAGING CONTRACT RISK

Most people involved in making and implementing business deals are *literate* in that they are able to read and write. Whether they are willing to use their literacy when it comes to contracts is another matter, as many business people are reluctant to read contracts. And we do not blame them. When under time pressure, one needs to prioritize, and today's commercial contracts are seldom reader-friendly documents where one can find required information quickly and easily. As we will see in the context of *lean contracting* and *contract visualization* later in this book, this may change with the development of more user-friendly contracts. Even without this change, if contract-related decisions are to be taken *knowingly*, contracts need to be read. But mere reading is obviously not enough— contracts need to be understood as well. To succeed in today's networked business, managers need to be *contractually literate*.

According to dictionary definitions, the word *literate* has two basic meanings: someone who can read and write and a well-informed, educated person. *Literacy* means the condition or quality of being literate or knowledgeable in a particular subject or field (for example, *computer literacy, financial literacy, health literacy, media literacy*). Contract literacy goes beyond having contracts or legal experts available when an issue arises.

Contract literacy starts with an understanding of the business and legal dimensions of contracts and the impact of contracts on successful business outcomes as well as the related risks. It involves recognizing contracts even when a document bearing such title is not present, and understanding when and how to read them. This requires a basic understanding of the laws that apply and are relevant to the company's business deals and relationships. Contract literacy enables business people to exercise informed judgment when negotiating and working with contracts, and knowing when professional legal help is required.

If we focus on the art of reading contracts in order to recognize contract risk, there are two principal aspects of *contract literacy*: being willing and able to read and understand (1) what the contract (even the small print) says and, often the more demanding task, (2) what it does *not* say but perhaps should. These aspects are presented in Figure 2.4 below.

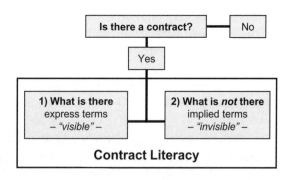

Figure 2.4   Contract literacy[12]

---

12   Siedel and Haapio 2011, p. 112; adapted from Haapio, H. (2006) Business success and problem prevention through proactive contracting. In P. Wahlgren and C. Magnusson Sjöberg (Eds.), *A Proactive Approach. Scandinavian Studies in Law*, Volume 49. Stockholm: Stockholm Institute for Scandinavian Law, pp. 149–94, 170, available at http://www.scandinavianlaw.se/pdf/49-9.pdf.

Both of the above aspects of *Contract Literacy* include additional factors, particularly in international business. Understanding what the contract says—the express terms—requires a good grasp of the language of the contract in question. Non-native speakers knowledgeable enough to deal with daily business correspondence and routines may not be able to fully understand the language and contents of contracts or the laws that apply to them.

Even native speakers (including lawyers) sometimes have trouble with legal terminology and concepts. Legal English is not the same throughout the world, and the meaning of concepts such as "consequential loss" or "force majeure" varies in different legal systems. In addition to mastering the relevant language and vocabulary, one often needs to master a number of abbreviations, such as the Incoterms trade terms, and their correct meaning and use. Some ordinary sounding words like "time is of the essence" may carry legal effect, and some terms may go unnoticed unless the reader has been educated to recognize them. Examples of key words and terms are discussed in Chapter 5 in connection with risky terms.

Often what is *omitted* from a contract is as important as (if not more important than) what is included. Understanding what the contract does *not* say and what that means requires a basic understanding of the relevant legal rules and principles as well as of trade usage and practices. The choice of law—as well as many other choices—may be made explicitly or implicitly.

Where no choice is made explicitly, a court or arbitral tribunal will apply choices made by default. For instance, if the parties have not specified the consequences of breach of contract, this does not mean that there will be no consequences if the innocent party suffers a loss and claims damages. Instead, the consequences (including damages) will be dictated by the applicable law, which might mean unlimited liability for the party breaching the contract. Or, to use another example, if the parties have not chosen to settle their possible disputes through arbitration, they may have inadvertently chosen litigation because once a dispute has arisen, it is more difficult to steer the dispute to mediation or arbitration. By making no explicit choices, the parties are assumed to have chosen the applicable law to provide the answer. This is why managers must understand the implied terms and default rules that will apply to their contracts. These are part of what we call "invisible" terms.[13]

Figure 2.4 illustrates another important requirement for contract literacy, namely that of being able to recognize a contract. This may sound trivial, but is not as easy as it sounds. As already stated, it is not always self-evident that people recognize that there is something "contractual" in documents such as a quotation, purchase order, confirmation, letter of intent, or memorandum of understanding. By the same token, some people tend to incorrectly believe that project plans, schedules, work scope definitions, technical specifications, drawings, etc., are "non-contractual," even when these are attached to a contract.

In addition to the "visible" and "invisible" terms, managers should have a basic understanding of the key variables that determine the sources of contract law. One of these relates to the subject of the contract. A real-estate contract, for instance,

---

13   For invisible terms more generally, see Haapio, H. (2004) Invisible terms in international contracts and what to do about them, *Contract Management*, July, 32–5, available at http://www.ncmahq.org/files/Articles/81EEB_cm_July04_32.pdf; Haapio, H. (2009) Invisible terms & creative silence: what you don't see can help or hurt you, *Contract Management*, September, 24–35, available at http://www.ncmahq.org/files/Articles/CM0909%20-%2024-35.pdf; and Haapio (2006).

might be governed by a different set of legal rules than a contract for the sale of goods, which in turn is governed by a different set of legal rules than a contract for the sale of services. Contracts for the sale of goods are further complicated by the fact that either a domestic law (for example, the Sale of Goods Act in the Nordic Countries or the Uniform Commercial Code in the United States) or an international law (the Convention on Contracts for the International Sale of Goods or CISG) might apply depending on whether the parties are in business, whether they are from different countries, whether and how the contract specifies the law governing the contract, and whether and how countries have adopted the CISG.[14]

In addition to specific laws governing the sale of goods, implied terms (or implied conditions) may be provided by general rules or principles of contract law. For example, most contracts contain a condition—often an invisible condition— along the lines that if one party does not perform, the other party does not have to perform either. Whether and how one party can excuse its performance using such a condition depends on which party was expected to perform first and what the contract requires. (For example, a notice of default is often required in such a situation.)

It is also important to understand that as a general principle a buyer is entitled to recover on a claim only if the supplier's alleged breach (such as delay or non-conformity) does not arise from a cause attributable to the buyer. This principle is expressed in the CISG, and it is also part of the UNIDROIT

---

14   The CISG can be found at http://www.cisg.law.pace.edu; for the declarations and reservations applicable to the adoption of the CISG made by various countries, see http://www.cisg.law.pace.edu/cisg/countries/cntries.html.

Principles of International Commercial Contracts[15] and of the Principles of European Contract Law.[16]

Freedom of contract is a fundamental principle of contract law. In business-to-business dealings, the parties can "write their own law" through their contract. However, managers should understand that this principle is subject to constraints that vary from one country to another. For example, there are legal doctrines that limit unfettered freedom of contract and set requirements regarding which commitments are legally binding and how contracts are formed.

In the business arena, the people developing tender and contract specifications or preparing proposals (a.k.a. bids, tenders, quotations and offers), purchase orders or order confirmations are seldom lawyers or contracts professionals. The same is true for people evaluating these documents and for those implementing the contracts that are made on their basis. They may be experienced, sophisticated, and business-savvy people, but their concerns are not primarily legal or contractual, and they may lack contract literacy. If this is the case, they are not likely to make full use of the power of their contracts. In order to identify and manage contract risks and opportunities, they need to become contractually literate.

---

15   The International Institute for the Unification of Private Law (UNIDROIT) (2010) *The UNIDROIT Principles of International Commercial Contracts*, available at http://www.unidroit.org/english/principles/contracts/principles2010/integralversionprinciples2010-e.pdf.
16   The Commission on European Contract Law, *The Principles of European Contract Law (PECL)*, available at http://www.law.kuleuven.be/web/mstorme/PECL.html and http://frontpage.cbs.dk/law/commission_on_european_contract_law.

SUMMARY

This chapter has discussed the reasons why companies make contracts and what we mean by "contract" and certain other terms used in this book. The chapter approaches contracts through their business and legal objectives and defines "contract risks" as risks that can lead to a negative deviation from the *expected outcomes of a contract*. In order to succeed in managing contract risks and opportunities and benefit from this chapter, you should:

1. View contracts as core business assets that require proactive management. Contracts are not merely legal tools that can be left to the lawyers alone.

2. Remember that *reaching business objectives* is the ultimate goal of contracts. Contract risks threaten the achievement of these objectives.

3. Plan contracting processes and documents using a holistic view and managerial–legal collaboration so that an overly legalistic view of contracts will not prevent your business from achieving its objectives. While the traditional legal emphasis remains important, it is no longer enough.

4. Become contractually literate because contract literacy is the foundation for identifying and managing contract risks and opportunities.

5. Learn to understand what the contract does *not* say and what that means. What is *omitted* can be as important as (if not more important than) what is included. Recognize and remove gaps in contracts, as these leave room for

invisible terms that may surprise you and your contracting partners.

6. Recognize and learn to use the promotive, preventive, and balancing power of contracts. Doing so will help you remove uncertainty and provide predictability in relation to both business and legal objectives and how the parties plan to work together to reach those objectives.

③ Sources of Contract Risk

No one can remain in business without making contracts. Yet entering a contract can be risky because it creates obligations. It also means relying on the other party to do (or refrain from doing) something, which in itself can give rise to many kinds of risk. This is a special concern when dealing with a supply chain, where one's own performance is dependent on the performance of others up and down the chain.

According to the ISO Risk Management Vocabulary (ISO Guide 73:2009), a *risk source* is an element that alone or in combination has the intrinsic potential to give rise to risk. Contracts themselves can be seen as sources of risk, but also as risk management tools. To find the true sources of contract risk and ways to respond to them, we need to look deeper than the mere making of contracts.

In this chapter, we look beyond contract wording to find the *real* sources of contract risk. We begin by exploring people's perceptions and choices and how they are (or are not) reflected in contracts. After introducing the contracting puzzle, we discuss the communication failures that easily occur when people from different functions and professions work together. In the sections that follow, we cover the reasons why some contract risks are unnoticed and unmanaged. Many of them do not show up on the risk registers, matrices, or logs commonly used in project management and organizational risk assessments.

LANGUAGE RISKS, CONTRACT WORDING, AND BEYOND

If one sees the contract as a legal document intended to regulate relationships through legal norms, the question of interpretation (and misinterpretation) quickly comes to mind. Where a dispute arises, the parties seldom concur on the terms of their agreement and what those terms mean. The language in their contract may be vague or ambiguous. The contract may include words or abbreviations or refer to standards the parties did not fully understand or take time to check. In international business, contracts are frequently written in English, even when it is not the native language of the parties. Contract structures, forms, and templates based on common law and Anglo-American style drafting have increasingly spread to civil law countries. Some of the concepts may not translate well into other languages and cultures, and "legal transplants" can cause confusion and add to the language risks.

Are issues around contract wording and interpretation a primary source of contract risk? Even though such issues frequently arise in court and arbitration, how often do they create risk in contracts? Experience tells us that risks and disputes seldom arise due to such issues alone. Contract wording and legal matters typically only become issues when business objectives are not reached, trust is eroded, the relationship does not work, and a business dispute cannot be resolved by non-legal means.

So in order to find the true sources of contract risk, we need to go beyond contract wording and legal issues to people and decision making—and not just rational decision making. Research and experience lead us to people's goals, perceptions, and emotional decision making, which often comes into play after they have faced a negative surprise or disappointment. Both in private life and in business, people decide to bring a claim or begin legal proceedings not only on rational decision criteria and the right to do so, but also on a *feeling of injury*. Louis M. Brown, known as the "Father of Preventive Law," once noted that legal claims and disputes usually do not arise because someone violates an agreement or a rule. Instead, they emerge because someone feels a sense of injury and is moved by circumstances to see it redressed.[1]

This is not to say that contract wording or legal issues or rules are not important. They are, especially when disputes are resolved through legal means. Understanding them is a central part of contract literacy, one of the foundations of contract risk management. Yet to understand the true causes of contract risk, we will first need to look into people's perceptions and choices and how they are (or are not) reflected in contracts.

---

1   Dauer, E.A. (2006) The role of culture in legal risk management. In P. Wahlgren and C. Magnusson Sjöberg (Eds.), *A Proactive Approach. Scandinavian Studies in Law*, Volume 49. Stockholm: Stockholm Institute for Scandinavian Law, pp. 93–108, 93–4, available at http://www.scandinavianlaw.se/pdf/49-6.pdf, citing Louis M. Brown, whose work has served as the foundational premise for the preventive aspects of the proactive approach.

PERCEPTIONS, GROWING COMPLEXITY, AND COMMUNICATION FAILURES

When making a contract, the responsibilities accepted and those entrusted to the other party are accepted and entrusted by choice—at least this is the assumption in most cases. Contracts are a record of what has been agreed. They should communicate the deal and its terms clearly so that future disputes over their meaning are avoided. If they do not, their language (and lack of language) can contribute to major misunderstandings and lead to false expectations and negative surprises.

An ideal contract matches the parties' business needs and reflects their true goals. Such a contract is capable of being implemented within the allotted time, with the resources that have been allocated, and within budget. The designed solution matches the priced solution, which in turn matches the solution that is described in the contract and will be implemented. Ideally, the supplied solution will meet the customer's requirements, while the project will satisfy the supplier's need for profitability and risk management.

With a complex project in mind, Figure 3.1 shows contracting as a puzzle of technical, implementation, business and legal parts, all of which must be consistent and coordinated. If—and only if—correctly assembled, the pieces of the puzzle form a complete, synchronized picture.

Capturing the required knowledge and crafting such contracts is seldom an easy task. The parts of the puzzle do not always fit together and create a successful business deal and relationship. Mindsets such as "contracts are legal documents," along with preconceptions and misconceptions, often prevent managers

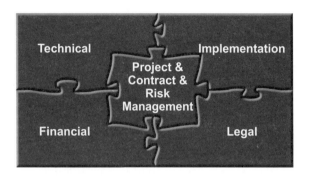

Figure 3.1   The contracting puzzle

and subject matter experts from contributing fully to the pre-contracting process and documents and later to the review of contract proposals and texts.

If management thinks that lawyers are in charge of contracts, the parties' goals and objectives, along with the technical and business aspects of contracts—and the related risks and how to respond to them—may receive too little attention. A lawyer not experienced in complex deals may see the legal element as if it is the whole puzzle and not just one piece. This can lead to failure of the lawyer to encourage people with knowledge about the scope, requirements, milestones, payments, dependencies, and so on, to join the team. The ultimate outcome is that some pieces of the contracting puzzle are missing, other pieces are not aligned and glued together properly and, when it comes to implementing the contract, the pieces will fall apart.

In complex projects, communication failures easily occur when people from different cultural and professional backgrounds work together. Problems may arise, for example, in relation to a technical specification or a statement of work. While these are key documents, they do not always receive the attention they deserve. Unless they are reviewed and aligned with the content of the remainder of the contract, inconsistencies and ambiguities can exist and cause problems during implementation. Even scope-related technical points should be expressed in a clear, concise way. This is as true in construction contracts as it is in technology contracts. Related to the latter, Mark Grossman, who has litigated many IT project disputes, once noted that a recurring reason for such disputes is communication failure, "which easily occurs when you have techies, business people, bean counters, and lawyers in one room pretending to speak the same language."[2]

Indeed, even if the people negotiating a contract share the same native language, they often only "pretend to speak the same language." Communication failures can occur inside and across multi-professional negotiating teams. These communication failures may lead to omitted and unaddressed issues and "self-evident" expectations that experts in the field feel no need to articulate. These can easily lead to disappointments and feelings of injury, bitter disputes, and contract interpretation issues. Another challenge in contracts is their growing complexity.

For a young lawyer just out of law school, the goal of contract drafting may be the creation of a legal masterpiece, a contract as close to "perfect" as possible: one that is legally binding, enforceable, and unambiguous, and provides solutions for all forseeable contingencies. In contrast, the business

2   Grossman, M. (2000) Contract negotiation crucial before website development. *The Miami Herald*, November 6, available at http://www.thsh.com/Publications/Articles-by-Topic/Technology-Telecom-and-Outsourcing/Contract-Negotiation-Crucial-Before-Website-deve.aspx.

community requires a different approach. According to a quotation attributed to Voltaire, "the perfect is the enemy of the good." Pursuing the "perfect" solution may end up being less beneficial than accepting a solution that is "good enough" and effective. Rather than perfect contracts, businesses need usable, operationally efficient contracts; these may be more helpful for achieving desired business goals and reasonable risk allocation at an acceptable cost. In fact, for businesses, successful implementation is the goal, not the contract itself. Signing a contract is just the beginning of the process of creating value,[3] so the core of contract drafting should be securing the *performance* the parties expect, not just a contract.

While many tend to favor plain language in contracts, conventional contract drafters still consider legalese superior. They talk about the benefits of language that has been "tested" and that has a clearly established, "settled" meaning. Change could be risky. But this is language that has been litigated and raises the question: why rely on language that resulted in litigation in the first place? Several studies confirm the benefits of plain language and its preference among different groups of readers—not only business users, but also lawyers and judges.

Contracts do not make things happen—*people* do. People need to follow the game plan that is spelled out in their contracts. But contracts are seldom easy for their users in the field, mostly non-lawyers, to understand and to implement. Their language and complexity may overload readers' cognitive abilities. If this happens and contract implementation fails, it would be wrong to assert that those contracts are "perfect" or even of reasonable quality, fit for their purpose. Quite the

---

3   Ertel, D. (2004) Getting past yes: negotiating as if implementation mattered. *Harvard Business Review*, 82(11), November, 60–8, p. 62.

opposite; even if they are legal masterpieces, they fall short of their ultimate purpose.

In the words of Professor Thomas D. Barton, Coordinator of the National Center for Preventive Law at California Western School of Law, one recurring barrier to successful contracting is the "exaggerated and largely unnecessary separation between the business goals that clients seek to achieve, and the legal methods by which contractual relationships are created and managed."[4] Adding to the challenges is the fact that year after year, contract drafters seem to add rather than remove text. The challenges of complexity are not limited to legal issues, of course. Contracts are created in a business environment that has become more complex.

As will be seen in the chapters that follow, *lean contracting* and *contract visualization* offer promising new ways that can provide clarity and ease of doing business while removing barriers that prevent contracts from being understood and used to their full potential. As stated in Chapter 1, management's attitude towards contracts determines how these new approaches will be used—or whether they are used at all.

GAPS IN THE CONTRACTING PROCESS— LACK OF CONTRACT MANAGEMENT

Even when contracts are as clear as possible, major issues can arise from a disconnect between the sales or procurement process and later implementation and management. After negotiating and signing, the parties should follow the plan

---

4   Barton, T.D. (2012) Collaborative contracting as preventive/proactive law. In G. Berger-Walliser and K. Østergaard (Eds.), *Proactive Law in a Business Environment*. Copenhagen: DJOF Publishing, pp. 107–27, 108.

embodied in their contract(s). People on the operational and delivery teams need information contained in contracts to coordinate in-house and outsourced functions, manage budget, scope, schedule, resources, and so on. In large, multi-locational organizations, the teams in charge of a project and the related contract(s) may change several times. Many businesses and people still do not see contracting as a process, but rather as a series of unconnected steps that result in the creation of a set of documents at some point and then delivery and implementation by an operational team only distantly, if at all connected, to the team that negotiated those documents. The lifecycle may consist of a series of fragmented activities rather than a managed process.

Figure 3.2 illustrates typical phases in a delivery project inside one organization. As illustrated in the figure, there may be several gaps in the project contract process that need to be bridged. These are often a reflection of the lack of contract management and accountability.

The picture becomes more complex when several organizations and supply chains—or several chains or networks forming an entire ecosystem—are added. Even in a "simple" two-party contract, the buyer's solicitation team and the supplier's

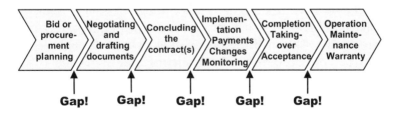

Figure 3.2   Mind the gaps in the contracting process!

proposal team may consist of people different from those on the contract negotiation team, none of whom may be part of the operational or delivery team. The teams may not meet and may just "inherit" from their predecessors the contract documents that they are expected to master and work with. Without guidance, delivering on the promises made in such documents is not easy.

On the sell-side, the operational team may need to implement the supply contract and to pass on to subcontractors the applicable terms (and risks) of that contract. This becomes especially complicated when dealing under global umbrella agreements—framework agreements made between group parent companies designed to be implemented at local level in several countries, all with their own jurisdictional, language, and other requirements.

CONTRACTUAL RISK ALLOCATION LEADING TO THE ILLUSION OF CONTROL WHERE NONE EXISTS

Some companies seem to believe that contract risk management involves using contract templates and terms that transfer all risks to the other party. This is especially true for large companies with strong bargaining power. Many are eager to transfer risk mechanically through onerous contracts. Some contractors accept such contracts trusting that they can transfer all risk down the procurement chain through back-to-back contracts with subcontractors and suppliers.[5] This

---

5   Back-to-back contracts are commonly used in construction and engineering projects throughout the world. See, for example, Zons, J. (2010) The minefield of back-to-back subcontracts. Part 1. *Construction Law International*, 5(1), March, 11–17; Zons, J. (2010) The minefield of back-to-back subcontracts. Part 2. *Construction Law International*,

practice is risky because, contrary to the company's intentions, it may become a source of risk and lead to negative surprises. The better suppliers may have a choice and, as a result of the onerous contract terms, may walk away and do business with the competition. Other companies may accept such terms trusting that they, in turn, can transfer them, along with the associated risk, to their business partners. So those onerous terms pass down the procurement chain until they reach a party with no bargaining power or will to fight.

While making other contract parties accept onerous terms might create a feeling of control and of having the risks addressed, the party down the supply chain may not be able to keep its promise. This, in turn, might cause everyone in the supply chain to suffer. If the breaching party is ultimately unable to carry the resulting losses, the risk may fall back on the shoulders of the company that thought others had assumed the risk. Effective contract risk management clearly requires a different approach.

In the context of today's networked businesses and contracts, a loss caused to a company, its contracting partner, or someone down the supply chain can impact all companies involved and their future collaboration. Expensive contractual disputes endanger relationships. Contract risk management must start with a realistic approach to risk, which often also requires a willingness to accept and share some risks. Making other parties over-promise or accept *any* terms may create an illusion of control where actually none exists. Everyone's fortunes in

---

5(2), June, 21–27; and Godwin, P., Roughton, D., Gilmore, D. and Kratochvilova, E. (2011) *Back-to-back Contracts*. Herbert Smith Freehills, April 15, available at http://www.lexology.com/library/detail.aspx?g=d75e0cf3-eb8d-4ce5-b39a-13e7b9b4ec4e.

a project are ultimately linked, and one party can never fully transfer risk to others in a supply chain.[6]

The problems of attempted risk allocation through one-sided contract terms is, of course, not limited to subcontractor situations and procurement chains. In some industries, suppliers still have the upper hand and will try to force their one-sided terms on their customers. Whether working on the sell-side or the buy-side, the truth remains that using contracts that attempt to transfer all risks to the other party does not make the risk go away and is no substitute for good risk management.

CURRENT CONTRACT PRACTICES—FOCUS ON WRONG ISSUES AND TERMS

Having strong contracts and legal resources along with approved contract terms and practices in place is generally a good thing, as is ensuring business controls and compliance. Yet these elements may have negative side effects in the form of increased bureaucracy and risk aversion. Rules in the contracting process that are too complicated can undermine productivity and threaten business performance. On the sell-side, this can lead to lost revenue, missed opportunities, and dissatisfied customers. In a survey related to sales contracting conducted by the International Association for Contract and Commercial Management (IACCM), a majority of the respondents felt that the contracting process fails in maximizing value, minimizing risk and assisting in the

---

6   Loosemore, M., Raftery, J., Reilly, C. and Higgon, D. (2006) *Risk Management in Projects*, 2nd edn. Abingdon: Taylor & Francis, p. 162. See also Loosemore, M. and McCarthy, C.S. (2008) Perceptions of contractual risk allocation in construction supply chains. *Journal of Professional Issues in Engineering Education and Practice*, 134(1), 95–105.

formation of strategic customer relationships. More than 40 percent of business people saw their sales contracts as a source of competitive *dis*advantage because these contracts are overly risk averse and impede would-be deals. If this perception is true, then today's contracting practices, while thought of as important for the management of risk, have in fact become a *source of risk*, resulting in potential loss or delay of business.[7]

The emphasis on the wrong things, including *risk allocation* (rather than *risk management*) is further reflected in IACCM annual surveys of negotiators—both sell-side and buy-side—from around the world. In these surveys, participants were asked to highlight the terms they negotiate with the greatest frequency. Year after year, two clauses have retained their # 1 and # 2 status: limitation of liability and indemnification. The results of IACCM's Tenth Annual Survey, 2011 Top Terms in Negotiation, are shown in the left column of the following table (Table 3.1):[8]

---

7   IACCM (2011a) *The State of Sales Contract Management*. International Association for Contract and Commercial Management, available at https://www.iaccm.com/ members/library/files/The_State_of_Sales_Contracting_Final.pdf. The report draws from input by more than 250 large corporations.

8   IACCM (2011b) *2011 Top Terms in Negotiation*. International Association for Contract and Commercial Management, available at https://www.iaccm.com/ members/library/files/top_terms_2011_1.pdf. According to the introduction, the results of this survey are based on input from more than 1,100 organizations, representing more than 8,000 negotiators. Individual contributors came from procurement, legal and sales contracting functions in more than 60 countries. Input typically represents large international corporations and therefore may not be an accurate reflection of negotiations at a local level or between smaller organizations.

Table 3.1   IACCM 2011 top terms in negotiation

	"Top Terms of Today" The terms that are negotiated with greatest frequency	"Top Terms of the Future" Terms which would be more productive in supporting successful relationships
1	Limitation of liability	Change management
2	Indemnification	Scope and goals
3	Price/charge/price changes	Responsibilities of the parties
4	Intellectual property	Communications and reporting
5	Payment	Performance/guarantees/undertakings
6	Liquidated damages	Limitation of liability
7	Performance/guarantees/undertakings	Delivery/acceptance
8	Delivery/acceptance	Dispute resolution
9	Applicable law/jurisdiction	Service levels and warranties
10	Confidential information/non-disclosure	Price/charge/price changes
11	Service levels and warranties	Audits/benchmarking
12	Warranty	Indemnification
13	Insurance	Intellectual property
14	Service withdrawal or termination	Payment
15	Data protection/security	Information access and management
16	Scope and goals	Business continuity/disaster recovery
17	Responsibilities of the parties	Applicable law/jurisdiction
18	Change management	Confidential information/non-disclosure
19	Invoices/late payment	Warranty
20	Audits/benchmarking	Assignment/transfer

The list of "Top Terms of Today" continues to be dominated by clauses dealing with the *consequences* of failure, claims and disputes, rather than on their *causes*—or on preventing them from happening again. What is shown in the left-hand column of Table 3.1 makes sense from a *risk allocation* point of view, but is clearly not optimal from a true *risk management* point of view.

The good news is that most negotiators recognize the need for a new negotiating agenda. In recent surveys, IACCM has asked participants to describe also where they think negotiating time should be focused in the future. The "Top Terms of the Future" listed in the right-hand column of Table 3.1 indicate that negotiators see a need to change their current agenda. They see more value in negotiating terms related to change management, scope and goals, and the parties' responsibilities than terms such as liability limitations and indemnities. The latter occupy the place they probably should—as last-resort fall-backs in the event that well-crafted intentions become derailed.[9]

SUMMARY

This chapter has discussed sources of contract risk, many of which are unrelated to contract terms and legal issues. One common denominator here is the human dimension, the way people perceive contracts and risks, and its impact on business use (or non-use) of contracts for risk and opportunity management. In order to identify and manage the *real* risks, you should:

---

9   See IACCM 2011b and IACCM (2009) The top negotiated terms: negotiators admit they are on wrong agenda. *Contracting Excellence*, July, available at http://www. iaccm.com/news/contractingexcellence/?storyid=923.

1. Use contract literacy to tackle the *real* sources or risk and *root causes* of problems first. Look beyond contract documents, language, and traditional risk sources. The *real* risks may not show on risk registers—especially if these deal mainly with risk allocation and liability issues. Identifying the real risks involves recognizing perceptions—your own and those of your team members—and making sure you all see the big picture.

2. Make sure that gaps in the contracting process, poor communication, or lack of proper contract management practices will not lead to unmanaged risks or opportunities.

3. Remember that risk *allocation* (as opposed to true risk *management*) may lead to the illusion of control where none exists.

4. Make sure your contracts focus on ways to enhance opportunities and increase the probability of positive outcomes rather than emphasizing the consequences of failure.

5. Instead of emphasizing contract clauses relating to liability limitations and indemnities, focus on a shared understanding of requirements and how they can be changed, along with provisions dealing with scope and goals, parties' responsibilities, and other Top Terms of the Future listed in the right-hand column of Table 3.1.

(4) Risks in Negotiating a Business Contract

Contract risk often focuses on the allocation of risks that arise during performance of a contract. As noted in Chapter 3, an IACCM survey indicates that a list of the top contract terms of today—that is, the terms negotiated with greatest frequency— is dominated by clauses that focus on the consequences of failure, claims and disputes. While these terms are important, negotiators should not overlook even greater risks that can be far more costly and, as we will see later, can even bankrupt a company.

In this chapter, we focus on the three main categories of these larger "big picture" risks: legal risks in contract formation, risks relating to negotiation strategy, and risks arising from overemphasis on legal concerns to the detriment of business goals. We first examine legal risks that arise in contract formation. Ignoring these risks can result in lost opportunities when legal requirements are not met or in liability when one side makes an unintended contractual commitment.

Second, we explore strategies designed to minimize the risk that negotiators will overlook an opportunity to create greater value that benefits both sides. Related to this risk is the importance of adopting an implementation mindset during contract negotiations.[1]

Third, we review the risks that arise when too much emphasis is placed on creating a legally perfect contract. This risk is illustrated by a recent situation in the United States where a company negotiated the sale of a property to a buyer for around $30 million. Signing the contract was delayed when the buyer's law firm insisted on including a clause that immunized the client from a low-probability risk. In the meantime, the seller found another buyer who was willing to pay over $100 million. The law firm's desire for a perfect legal contract resulted in its client losing over $70 million in value! This chapter introduces lean contracting as a method that enables the development of contracts that are management as well as legal tools.

The chapter concludes with discussion of a management tool that is very useful when you are faced with negotiation decisions that are affected by risk and uncertainty.

LEGAL RISKS IN CONTRACT FORMATION

In this section, we cover the key legal concerns relating to contract formation that represent the foundation of contract literacy. Before doing so, however, we cover a preliminary matter relating to the source of contract law.

---

1   The second and third parts of this chapter have been adapted in part from Siedel, G.J. and Haapio, H. (2010) Using proactive law for competitive advantage. *American Business Law Journal*, 47(4), 641–86.

THE SOURCE OF CONTRACT LAW

In our globalized economy, contract law has become increasingly similar from country to country, but differences still exist. Because these differences relate to the source of contract law, understanding the source is an important attribute of contract literacy. As a result, at the beginning of any negotiation you should determine whether your situation is governed by the laws of a civil law or common law country.

The distinction between civil law and common law countries is especially important because the legal requirements for a valid contract differ to some extent. For example, civil law does not include the consideration requirement discussed below.

Generally speaking, civil law countries include continental European countries and the former colonies of these countries. In civil law countries, the principles of law are primarily found in a published "code"—in effect, an encyclopedia of law. Common law countries (generally England and its former colonies) rely more heavily on previously decided cases—that is, precedents—as a source of law. Apart from differences in legal requirements, one practical distinction between the two legal systems is that common law contracts tend to be quite lengthy because lawyers attempt to anticipate every possible scenario that might arise when a contract is performed. Civil law contracts traditionally were shorter because the contract could incorporate provisions from the code. However, even in civil-law countries there is a trend toward longer contracts.

THE KEY LEGAL ELEMENTS IN CONTRACT FORMATION

We now turn to the foundation of contract literacy—the key legal elements necessary to create a contract. These elements in effect represent a checklist for use in your future negotiations.

1. *Agreement.* The requirement that parties reach an agreement is fairly straightforward. One party makes an offer; the other party accepts the offer. In many cases, common sense should tell you whether a contract has been formed, as illustrated by facts derived from a case in China. A store sent an offer to purchase televisions to a manufacturer, with delivery to be made to the store. The manufacturer sent a reply accepting the offer, but added that the store had to pick up the televisions at the factory. In its response, the store agreed to pick them up at the factory. When the price of televisions dropped, the store claimed that there was no contract. Was the store correct?

A common sense analysis is that the store first made an offer but that the manufacturer's so-called "acceptance" was not a legal acceptance because it changed the terms of the offer by changing the place of delivery. This made the manufacturer's communication a counter offer, which was accepted by the store. So there was a contract as of the date of this final communication.

A situation entailing a much higher degree of risk can arise when parties use preliminary documents during contract negotiations. This type of document, often called a memorandum of understanding, a letter of intent or an agreement in principle, is useful in complex negotiations when the two sides have difficulty in reducing their negotiated agreement to writing.

However, these documents carry a major risk. If the parties do not document their intent not to be legally bound until a contract is signed, at some point, as the parties fill in the missing parts, the document might become detailed enough for a court to conclude that it represents a binding contract.

This risk might also affect third parties. For example, several years ago, Pennzoil negotiated a memorandum of agreement to acquire Getty Oil. When Texaco later entered into a separate contract to purchase Getty Oil, Pennzoil claimed that its memorandum of agreement was actually a binding contract and that Texaco's actions interfered with its contract rights. In a subsequent trial, the jury agreed with Pennzoil in deciding that Texaco owed $10.5 billion in damages. When this judgment drove Texaco into bankruptcy, the two companies reached a settlement agreement whereby Texaco paid Pennzoil "only" $3 billion.

While they are useful negotiating tools, preliminary documents can result in significant risks for the parties negotiating the agreement or for third parties like Texaco. To minimize these risks, you should carefully spell out in the document that it is for negotiating purposes only and is not a final contract until you so agree.

2. *Consideration.*   Consideration is required in common law systems. While consideration has a technical legal definition, in everyday language it means that for a deal to be legally binding, both sides must give up something. For example, if a university graduate promises to donate $20 million to her university in a written signed agreement, the agreement is not binding unless the university promises to give up something in return.

In most business transactions, consideration is not a concern because both sides give up something—one side gives up a service or a product and the other side gives up payment. However, the risk of not meeting the consideration requirement increases when a contract is modified. For instance, assume that you, as a contractor, agree to remodel a building for a customer by a certain date. At your request, the customer agrees to give you a one-month extension, but you do not give the customer anything in exchange for this extension. Technically, the customer's agreement is not binding and you could be sued for breach of contract if you did not complete performance by the original date—unless you provided consideration for the one-month extension.

3. *Legality*.   A contract that calls for the violation of a law is not enforceable. In many cases—for example, a contract to sell illegal drugs—this element is easy to understand. In other situations, where there might be a violation of public policy, the law is more complex.

For instance, your company might decide to protect confidential information by requiring employees to sign so-called non-compete agreements stating that they cannot work for a competitor within three years after leaving your company. In some countries this non-compete agreement might be illegal because it restricts the ability of your employees to obtain employment. And even where the agreement is legal, in common law countries the consideration element would require your company to give something to employees in exchange for their signing the non-compete agreement.

4. *Writing*.   Both civil law and common law countries have rules providing that certain contracts must be in writing to be enforceable. These rules carry a huge financial risk when

you make a wrong assumption about whether a writing is required, with the result that you miss a business opportunity (because you thought that your oral agreement was binding) or create an unintended liability (because you thought that your oral agreement was not binding).

As a result, you should never enter into a contract negotiation without understanding the applicable rules regarding whether a writing is required. But your understanding of the law should be supplemented by a practical strategy: during negotiations make it clear that you are not bound until a written agreement is made.

In other words, all of your agreements should be in writing. There are two reasons for this advice. First, by placing your agreement in writing you will not have to worry about the legal complexity of determining whether the agreement must be written. Second, and perhaps more important, you will avoid the consequences of memory failure. That is, even when the law allows oral contracts, the two sides to a contract will often have different recollections of the details of their agreement. Their views might differ as to key issues—such as who the parties are, when the agreement starts, how long it continues to be in force, and when and how it can be terminated. These memory problems are avoided when the agreement is written and addresses the key issues. As noted by a Chinese proverb, even the palest ink is better than the best memory.

But another legal concern creates a separate risk once you reduce your agreement in writing. To illustrate this concern, we might assume that you have just been hired by a company in a city distant from your own. During negotiations, the company promises to pay for your moving costs but, when the agreement is put into writing, this promise is not included.

Are you legally entitled to moving costs, assuming that the company admits that it made the promise?

The answer varies depending on country law. Under the law of some countries, a rule called the Parol Evidence Rule states that once you have put your agreement into writing, evidence of prior or contemporaneous agreements (such as the company's promise to pay moving costs) cannot be introduced as evidence if you decide to sue the company. This rule makes sense in that during a negotiation both sides might make many agreements that they later cast aside and don't intend to incorporate into the final agreement. If the court allowed them to bring evidence of these agreements into court instead of relying on the final, written document, courts would forever be reviewing and attempting to untangle the details of negotiations.

Even when you are negotiating a deal under the laws of a country that *has not* adopted the Parol Evidence Rule, it is likely that your contract will include a provision stating that the rule applies. These provisions appear under a variety of headings—for example, merger clause, integration clause, or entire agreement clause—and usually read as follows: "This agreement constitutes the entire agreement between the parties related to the subject matter and supersedes all prior representations, agreements, negotiations or understandings, whether oral or in writing." For this reason, you always should read your contracts before signing them to make sure that the writing matches the agreement that you negotiated.

In following this advice, keep in mind that even in countries that *have* adopted the Parol Evidence Rule, it might not apply in all situations. For example, the United States has adopted the rule but has also adopted the Convention on Contracts for the International Sale of Goods (CISG), which does not include the rule. So if you enter into a contract for the international sale of goods governed by the CISG, evidence of prior agreements might be admissible in court unless you include a merger clause that clearly states that evidence outside the written contract is not admissible.

5. *Authority.* The final element necessary to create a legally binding contract is authority. In other words, does the party with whom you are negotiating have authority to make the contract? This is always the first question that you should raise when negotiating a contract because, if there is no authority, your negotiation might be a waste of time.

When you negotiate with someone who claims to represent a principal, there are three types of authority that the purported agent might possess. As illustrated by Figure 4.1, they are express authority, implied authority and apparent authority.

Express authority is created when the principal states that the agent has authority to negotiate a contract. *Implied* authority arises from the position held by the agent. It is implied that agents in certain positions have authority to enter into certain types of contracts. For example, it is implied that individuals

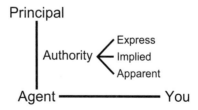

Figure 4.1   The three types of authority

hired as purchasing agents have authority to purchase goods within normal limits on behalf of the company.

Apparent authority arises when the principal leads you to believe that there is authority when there is none. For example, the principal might send you a letter of authority stating that the agent has authority to make purchases on behalf of the principal. If the principal limits the agent's authority without telling you, you could hold the principal liable because the agent would have apparent authority.

A situation based on a court case illustrates why authority is important. An employee wanted to borrow money from a bank for personal purposes, but had no collateral to secure the loan. So the bank asked for a loan guarantee from the employee's company. The company's general manager visited the bank and signed the guarantee on behalf of the company—and the guarantee stated that he had authority to do so. When the employee later defaulted on the loan, the bank sued the company on the basis of its guarantee but lost. The court concluded that the company had not given the general manager express authority to guarantee employees' personal loans. Implied authority was missing because guaranteeing employee personal loans is not something that general managers normally do. And there was no evidence of apparent authority.

In this case, the bank created unnecessary risk because it relied on the general manager's guarantee that he had authority. The important risk avoidance message is that if in doubt, and especially when dealing with guarantees or other major commitments that do not fall within the scope of your counterparty's representative's day-to-day duties, verify the authority of the person with whom you are negotiating.

The company should have asked the principal (which in this case would be the company board of directors) whether the agent had authority and should not have relied on the agent's statements about authority.

RISKS RELATING TO NEGOTIATION STRATEGY AND CONTRACT IMPLEMENTATION

A major and often overlooked risk arises when contract negotiators, in their zeal to claim value for themselves, overlook opportunities to create value that will improve results for both sides. We will first describe a negotiation exercise entitled "The House on Elm Street" (which is used by one of the authors in classes for business executives and MBA students) to illustrate a strategy for minimizing this risk. In essence, this strategy requires moving from a position-based to an interest-based negotiation strategy. We will then examine another major and costly negotiation risk that arises when there is a separation between a deal-making and a deal-implementation mindset.

MISSING VALUE-CREATING OPPORTUNITIES DURING THE NEGOTIATION PROCESS

In simplified form, the House exercise involves a negotiation between the owner of an old Victorian house that has a large back yard and a company that wants to purchase the house, tear it down, and use part of the back yard for extra parking. The seller needs at least $150,000 for the house so she can purchase an assisted living apartment designed for senior citizens. She is proud of the house and wants the buyer to preserve it.

Because of concerns that the owner might not sell to a company that wants to tear down the house, the buyer negotiates through a secret agent. (That is, the seller thinks that the agent is buying the house for family purposes and does not realize that the agent represents the company.) The buyer is in the business of constructing assisted living apartments designed for senior citizens and has a large inventory of unsold apartments. It is willing to pay up to $250,000 for the house.

When this exercise is debriefed in class, the results are predictable. Students acting in the roles of buyer and seller focus on price (sellers obviously want a high price for the property and buyers want to pay a low price) and they typically negotiate deals that range from $150,000 to $250,000, with results clustering around $170,000. They are then asked to consider an alternative strategy that focuses on identifying the interests of each side and builds on those interests to create value. This is the philosophy advocated in the classic book *Getting to Yes* by Fisher, Ury and Patton.[2]

When they move beyond the position-based focus on *what* the other side wants (high price versus low price) to the interest-based focus on *why* the other side is making its demands, they realize that the seller needs the purchase price to acquire an assisted living apartment and that buyer can meet this need with one of its large stock of empty apartments. They also realize that the buyer can meet its real estate needs by using only a portion of the back yard without tearing down the house, which is important to the seller. As a result, the seller can obtain an apartment worth more than what she could acquire for the typical negotiated purchase price of $170,000, while the buyer's purchase price is reduced because its building

---

2   Fisher, R., Ury, W. and Patton, B. (1991) *Getting to Yes: Negotiating Agreement Without Giving In*, 2nd edn. New York, NY: Penguin Group.

costs are less than the value of the apartment to the seller. The buyer is also better off with this solution because it can sell the house and the unused portion of the yard to a family, thus reducing its costs further. So, through the adoption of an interest-based strategy, the results are better for both sides.

In order for this strategy to succeed the two sides should attempt to avoid being trapped by the mythical fixed pie assumption. As articulated by Harvard professor Max Bazerman,[3] negotiators often assume that they are fighting over a fixed pie and that their interests are in direct conflict. By focusing on interests, participants in the House exercise realize that not all interests are in conflict: the seller needs an assisted living apartment and the buyer can easily meet this need. As a result they can create a larger pie that benefits both sides.

DISTINCTION BETWEEN DEAL-MAKING AND DEAL-IMPLEMENTATION MINDSETS

Many organizations adopt a deal-maker approach in contract negotiations that separates contract formation from contract implementation. In the words of Danny Ertel,

> *An organization that embraces the deal maker approach ... tends to structure its business development teams in a way that drives an ever growing stream of new deals. ... But they also become detached from implementation and are likely to focus more on the agreement than on its business impact.*[4]

---

3   Bazerman, M.H. (1994) *Judgment in Managerial Decision Making*, 3rd edn. New York, NY: John Wiley.
4   Ertel, D. (2004) Getting past yes: negotiating as if implementation mattered. *Harvard Business Review*, 82(11), November, 60–8, p. 62.

Just as organizations adopt a deal-maker mindset, individuals within an organization who negotiate contracts can slip into a deal-maker mindset as their competitive instincts (fuelled by the mythical fixed pie assumption) emerge during a negotiation. One of the consequences of this mindset can be a focus on clauses dealing with liabilities and risk allocation. Other consequences noted by Ertel include the prevalence of positional bargaining tactics such as using surprise to gain advantage, holding back information, and setting false deadlines to close deals.[5]

These deal-making tactics might produce a contract that, while it looks good on paper, inhibits the relationships necessary to successfully implement the contract. Given the ascendancy of business models that are built on relationships, negotiators who can move from a deal-making to an implementation mindset have an opportunity to minimize the risk of contract failure, thus creating competitive advantage for their companies. Among the characteristics of the new mindset described by Ertel are a focus on the end of the deal, the identification of obstacles to successful completion, and a willingness to help the other side prepare for the negotiation, including consideration of implementation concerns.[6]

An implementation mindset is especially useful in identifying the parties' often unrecognized and unexpressed expectations. For instance, by asking simple questions during the deal-making stage, both sides can specify and align needs, establish expectations, and clarify the scope of solutions in a manner that can minimize the risk of major business and legal problems later on.

---

5   Ertel 2004, p. 65.
6   Ertel 2004, p. 63.

An implementation mindset is consistent with the IACCM survey described in Chapter 3, in which participants were asked to describe not only what they spend most time on in negotiating deals today, but also where they think negotiating time should be focused in the future. The "Top Terms of the Future" listed in that chapter indicate that negotiators see more value in negotiating terms relating to change management, scope and goals, and the parties' responsibilities than terms such as liability limitations and indemnities.

The top terms of the future are dominated by the need for clarity about the basic intentions of the parties, and the need to ensure that the deal remains on track and can be adjusted in the face of changing conditions or requirements. With a revised focus on these terms of the future, the parties can attempt to establish procedures for more open information flows and greater transparency, thus signaling their intent to collaborate and work together to manage risks and optimize results.

Another aspect of the implementation mindset relates to the evaluation of negotiation success. As Ertel notes, rather than focusing in their evaluations on whether they achieved price discounts, purchasers should emphasize a full-cost approach that considers matters such as "the operating efficiencies gained through using the supplier, the reductions in defects achieved by the supplier, and even the supplier's role in developing product or service innovations." And rather than focusing on sales volume, sellers should emphasize "the longevity of their customer relationships, the innovations that have resulted from their interactions with customers ... and the referral business that can be traced to those customers."[7]

---

7   Ertel, D. (1999) Turning negotiation into a corporate capability. *Harvard Business Review*, 77(3), May–June, 55–70, p. 62.

RISKS RESULTING FROM ATTEMPTING TO CREATE A LEGALLY PERFECT CONTRACT

The first part of this chapter focuses on legal risks in forming a contract and discusses elements of contract literacy that must be understood by every negotiator. While these elements are important in enabling you to secure a sound legal foundation for achieving your contractual goals and to avoid becoming burdened with unwanted contractual commitments, other risks arise when too much emphasis is placed on creating legally perfect contracts.

In basic terms a business-to-business contract is defined as a value-creating agreement that is enforceable by law. Lawyers traditionally have focused on the enforceability component of this definition by thinking of the contract as a legal tool as they attempt to construct airtight agreements that maximize their clients' legal rights and minimize legal risk. The lawyers' orientation is not surprising given their mindset. Lawyers are trained to look at contracts through the eyes of a judge who might eventually have to rule on a contract dispute. Thus a good contract, from the lawyers' perspective, is one that is enforceable.

While the "enforceable by law" part of the business contract definition is important and cannot be ignored, legal enforceability must be balanced with the "value-creating agreement" part of the definition. In other words, while clients want their agreements to be enforceable, they also want contracts that enable them to achieve their business goals by serving as a management tool as well as a legal tool. As law professors Ian Macneil and Paul Gudel note in their book *Contracts: Exchange Transactions and Relations*, "[o]nly lawyers and other trouble-oriented folk look on contracts primarily as a source of trouble and disputation, rather than a way of getting things done."[8]

A lean contracting strategy enables managers, along with their lawyers, to minimize legal complexity in their contracts. This strategy applies lean production concepts to the "production" of contracts by asking whether company contracts can be simplified through an examination of the costs and benefits of various contract clauses. For example, the in-house legal team at the brewer Scottish & Newcastle sensed that company resources were being wasted in the contract negotiation process. Their work in developing what they called the Pathclearer approach to commercial contracting—and what we call lean contracting—illustrates the benefits that are possible from reorienting contracting strategy.

The lawyers initially asked three fundamental questions. First, what is the purpose of a contract? In answering this question, they developed a traditional definition of a legal contract:[9]

> [T]he only purpose of a contract, as opposed to a general statement of what a business intends to do with its business partners, is to ensure that rights and obligations which the parties agree to can be enforced in court (or arbitration). Put even more bluntly, the essence of a contract is the ability to force someone else to do something they don't want to do, or to obtain compensation for their failure.

8   Macneil, I.R. and Gudel, P.J. (2001). *Contracts—Exchange Transactions and Relations. Cases and Materials*, 3rd edn. New York, NY: Foundation Press, pp. vii–viii.
9   All quotations in this section are from Weatherley, S. (2005) Pathclearer—A more commercial approach to drafting commercial contracts. *PLC Law Department Quarterly*, October–December, 39–46, available at http://www.iaccm.com/loggedin/library/nonphp/pathclearer article pdf.pdf and at http://www.clarity-international.net/documents/Pathclearer%20article%20in%20PLC-3.pdf.

With this definition in mind, they realized that certain terms, including price and product specifications, should always be captured in writing and that certain types of deals, such as "share purchases, loan agreements, and guarantees," require detailed written contracts. But they also realized that many other scenarios—for instance, a long-term relationship between a customer and supplier—call for a "much lighter legal touch." Realizing that in these situations the consequences of forcing contractual obligations on an unwilling partner through "begrudging performance" or litigation are not attractive, they concluded that leaving long-term relationships "to the irresistible forces of free market economics [is better than an] attempt to place continuing contractual obligations on each other." In other words, freedom of the market should dominate the traditional freedom of contract philosophy that has led to detailed written contracts.

Their second of the three fundamental questions focused on the risks associated with traditional, law-oriented contracts: "What are the drawbacks of detailed written contracts?" In answering this question, the in-house lawyers reached a number of insightful conclusions. First, "[t]he apparent certainty and protection of a detailed written contract ... [are] often illusory" and wasteful as companies pay their lawyers first for drafting contracts that only the lawyers understand and second for interpreting what the contracts mean. The in-house legal team witnessed "bizarre attempts" by lawyers attempting to reach certainty, such as "external lawyers spending hours drafting and debating the precise legal definition of beer for insertion in a simple beer supply agreement." They also recognized the futility of trying to predict the future.

Their second conclusion was that detailed contracts generate disputes rather than avoiding them.

> *Without a detailed contract, business people who become involved in a dispute will generally discuss the issue and reach a sensible agreement on how to resolve it. ... However, where a detailed contract exists, the same parties will feel obliged to consult their lawyers.*

Third, the complexity of such contracts causes confusion and the risk that the parties will be unable to focus on key terms because it becomes "difficult to see the wood for the trees."

Fourth, the general law of contracts provides "a fair middle-ground solution to most issues" and "[t]he beauty of simply relying on the 'general law,' rather than trying to set out the commercial arrangement in full in a detailed written contract, is that there is no need to negotiate the non-key terms of a deal."

Fifth, negotiating detailed written contracts is expensive in terms of management and lawyer time and delayed business opportunities.

Finally, detailed written contracts can also cause the parties to focus on worst-case scenarios that "can lead to the souring of relationships. ... [C]ontinuing business relationships are like butterflies. They are subtle and hard to capture. When you do try to nail them down, you can kill them in the process."

The third and final question the in-house legal team asked is whether there are other ways to achieve business goals without detailed written contracts. The Scottish & Newcastle lawyers answered this question in the affirmative by focusing on the concept of "commercial affinity," the force that keeps parties together in "mutually beneficial commercial relationships." The alignment of the parties' interests through carefully constructed incentives, combined with the right of either side to walk away from the deal if it ceases to be economically attractive, incentivizes them to meet the other side's needs and alleviates the need for "a myriad of tactical rights and obligations in a contract."

In summary, the Scottish & Newcastle lawyers realized that a different approach is appropriate "when the parties are in a continuing business relationship, rather than just carrying out a snapshot transaction" that might require a detailed written contract. They did not advocate a complete return to handshake agreements. For instance, "exit arrangements (such as obligations to buy dedicated assets from the supplier ...) do need to be spelled out in the contract." But by addressing the three fundamental questions, they realized that in many other situations leaner contracts were possible.

The company's Pathclearer approach in a continuing business relationship is illustrated by the lean contract that the company negotiated with a service provider. The two parties originally had a ten-year contract that ran over 200 pages. During contract renegotiation, they substantially reduced the size of the contract through the Pathclearer approach by giving each party the right to terminate after 12 months' notice—a mutual "nuclear button."

> By giving ourselves the ability to terminate at any time, we avoided the need to have to negotiate detailed terms in the contract. ... This is a much more powerful way of influencing the service provider than

a technical debate over whether they were complying
with the words set out in the contract.

Even when parties conclude that a detailed written contract is necessary, they might eliminate certain provisions that create inefficient contract negotiations. For example, Microsoft included an indemnity provision in its contracts that caused many contract negotiations to last an additional 60 to 90 days because customers did not like the clause. Microsoft softened the provision after realizing that the benefits of the clause were minimal in contrast to potential costs that included reputational costs (resulting from confrontational negotiations), resource costs (lawyer and management time) and cash flow costs (caused by delayed sales during the additional two to three months of contract negotiation).

In describing and commenting on these costs, Tim Cummins, CEO of the IACCM, concluded that "[r]isk management is about balancing consequence and probability. Here is an example where consequence was managed without regard to probability—and as a result, other risks and exposures [such as reputational and resource costs] became inevitable."[10]

A DECISION-MAKING TOOL FOR ADDRESSING RISK DURING THE CONTRACTING PROCESS

When negotiating business deals, negotiators often face difficult choices that depend on their evaluation of risk. Consider, for example, this dilemma faced by your company

---

10   This example is drawn from Cummins, T. (2006) Best practices in commercial contracting. In P. Wahlgren and C. Magnusson Sjöberg (Eds.), *A Proactive Approach. Scandinavian Studies in Law*, Volume 49. Stockholm: Stockholm Institute for Scandinavian Law, pp. 131–47, 138, available at http://www.scandinavianlaw.se/pdf/49-8.pdf.

in deciding to acquire either Company A or Company B.[11] Company A has a $21 million value while Company B has a $15 million value. If the purchase price is the same for both companies, the decision to acquire Company A would be easy.

However, two risks arise if you acquire Company A. First, there is a 90 percent chance that the government will challenge the acquisition. Second, there is a 60 percent chance that the government will win. If the government wins, the value of Company A drops to $14 million. Even if the government loses, the value drops to $19 million because of legal costs incurred in fighting the government. The government will not challenge the acquisition of Company B.

Assuming that you will base your decision solely on the valuation of the two companies after factoring in risk, would you decide to acquire Company A or B? Most decision makers faced with this dilemma intuitively choose B. The decision tree is a tool that can help you determine whether this is a good decision.

A decision tree looks like a tree on its side. Decisions are represented by boxes. As depicted in Figure 4.2, the decision in this case is whether to acquire Company A or B. Uncertainties are shown as circles. The two uncertainties in this situation are: (1) Will the government challenge the acquisition, and (2) if there is a challenge, will the government win?

After drawing the tree, probabilities are added (that is, 90 percent chance that the government will challenge the acquisition and 60 percent chance that the government

11   This example is described in Victor, M.B. (1978) Predicting the cost of litigation. *Strategy & Leadership*, 6(6), 15–18.

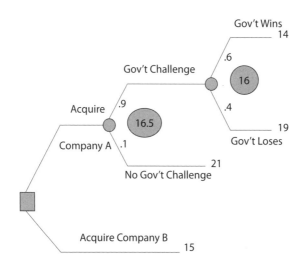

Figure 4.2   Using a decision tree to calculate the impact of risk

will win). Endpoint values are also inserted: the valuation of Company A under three scenarios and the valuation of Company B. Finally an expected value of Company A is determined by calculating weighted averages: 60 percent of $14 million plus 40 percent of $19 million is $16 million, and 90 percent of $16 million plus 10 percent of $21 million is $16.5 million. Thus, the expected value of acquiring Company A ($16.5 million) is higher than the value of Company B ($15 million) and, if the decision is made on this basis alone, you should acquire Company A.

Decision trees can also be used to make other contract risk-related decisions. Even simple "back-of-the-envelope" calculations using decision trees can make the available choices visible and easier to prioritize.

For instance, in the example above, Tim Cummins of IACCM described Microsoft's decision whether to insist on an indemnity clause in its contracts. As he noted, the indemnity clause brought minimal benefits in contrast to costs that included resource expenses (lawyer and management time) and lost cash flow (caused by delayed sales during the additional two to three months of contract negotiation).

Decision trees are useful in visualizing and testing decisions like the one that Microsoft faced. Let's assume that the contract clause in question provided Microsoft with $20 million in indemnity and that there is a 1 percent chance that it will lose $20 million and invoke the clause. (This probability should be easy to estimate based on past experience. In practice, the chance that such a clause would be invoked is probably less than 1 percent.) Let's also assume that the resource costs and cash flow costs to obtain the indemnity are $1 million. In effect, Microsoft would pay $1 million for the equivalent of a $20 million insurance policy. Given these assumptions, should Microsoft pay $1 million for this "insurance"?

The decision tree in Figure 4.3 depicts the 1 percent chance that Microsoft will lose $20 million if it drops the indemnification clause demand and the 99 percent chance that it will lose nothing. This results in an expected value of –$200,000 (0.99 × 0 plus 0.01 × $2 million). Based on these assumed values and probabilities (and not factoring in its attitude toward risk), Microsoft made a good decision when it dropped its demand for an indemnification clause, because the $1 million cost is $800,000 higher than the –$200,000 expected value of dropping the clause.

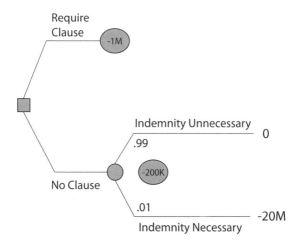

Figure 4.3   Using   a   decision   tree   to   make   an indemnification clause decision

SUMMARY

This chapter has examined three categories of risk that, while often overlooked in contract risk analysis, carry the potential for huge losses. In order to benefit from the concepts discussed in this chapter, you should:

1. Achieve contract literacy by understanding the key elements that are required for the formation of a legally binding contract. This understanding should help you avoid the risk that the value you hope to achieve in your contracts will not be legally secure or that you will become entangled in an unwanted contractual commitment.

2. Use an interest-based negotiation strategy that, instead of asking the other side what they want, focuses on why they

want it. You should also make sure that your negotiation team's mindset focuses on implementation rather than deal-making alone.

3. Create contracts that are useful management tools rather than only legal tools. The lean contracting practices described in this chapter should enable you to focus on your business goals rather than on creating a legally perfect contract.

4. When faced with negotiation decisions that are impacted by risk and uncertainty, use a decision tree or other visual tools introduced later in this book to clarify your options.

⑤ Risky Terms and Issues in Contracts

As seen in earlier chapters, contract risks can take many forms and arise from many different sources. This chapter covers the risks inherent in a contract itself. Many "risky" terms and issues, such as the dynamics of price and payment on one hand and work, key performance indicators, and acceptance criteria on the other hand are deal-, industry- and situation-specific. In the following sections, we will focus on terms and issues that are more universal.

We first examine contract terms that deal with risk and the most frequent sources of claims and disputes. We then divide contract clauses into two groups, *active clauses* and *passive clauses*, and explore their interrelationship, along with related performance and legal concerns. We then introduce, with examples, typical high-risk issues and risky clauses in contracts. These clauses are frequently used by parties as *risk allocation* or *risk transfer* mechanisms in contracts. To succeed in *contract risk management*, both parties need to be aware of the existence of these mechanisms so they can make better risk-related decisions and share and manage risk together.

WHICH CONTRACT TERMS DEAL WITH RISK?

When asked about contract terms that deal with risk or are helpful in managing risk, people tend to think about limitations of liabilities, indemnities, and the like—or clauses that specifically mention the word "risk," such as clauses dealing with owner's or contractor's risk in construction contracts or the risk of loss of or damage to the goods in sales contracts. Many seem to think that these are the *only* contract terms that deal with risk. Such a view is too narrow.

In truth, *all* contract terms deal with risk. Contracts are made to reach business and project objectives, and the success in reaching these objectives is dependent on issues such as price, scope, performance undertakings, acceptance criteria, and the management of change. On the sell-side, future profitability depends on these issues. The risk of not getting paid at all or on time, the risk to cash flow, and the risk of diminishing margin all depend on contracts. On the buy-side, contracts are the foundation achieving the expected benefits. The right contract structure and terms can make all the difference between success and failure, profit and loss, margin improvement and margin erosion—even customer/supplier satisfaction and disappointment, the latter possibly leading to claims and disputes.

So risk is not dealt with only in what some might call the "legal parts" of contracts addressing liabilities, remedies, and contingencies. Nor is risk addressed only in the boilerplate provisions, standard terms and conditions, or the small print. Apart from these clauses, technical specifications, work scope definitions, service descriptions, and other deal-specific provisions and attachments deal with risk. Dealing with risk is also embedded in decisions related to contract type, structure, and model, which in turn are determined by the industry and business at hand. For example, when choosing their contract pricing model, such as the choice between *fixed price* and *time and materials*, businesses deal with risk. They also deal with risk when agreeing on each party's obligations, roles, and responsibilities and how these are timed. Who has to bear what risks also depends on what role a company takes and where it is located in a supply chain, which at the same time is a contract chain.

In many cases, the "non-legal parts" dealing with scope, requirements, key performance indicators, acceptance criteria, completion, acceptance, warranties, availability, performance, and payment (whether advance payments are made, whether bonds or guarantees are involved, what their terms are, and so on) contain the true sources of risk—and risk control mechanisms. For example, as we will see later in this chapter, a major difference in the risks of both parties depends on whether a service provider agrees to provide a specific result or only to make certain resources available.

While certain "risky" clauses dealing with, for instance, liability or remedies are quite easy to spot, as we will see later, the risks embedded in the *absence* of certain clauses need to be recognized as well. Apart from the express, "visible" terms of a contract, the default rules also deal with risk. They enter the picture if the parties do not provide a different solution in their contract. If the parties want to limit liabilities or remedies, they can do so in their contract. If they don't, they need to be aware of "invisible" terms that do not provide limitations. The lack of express contractual limitations can lead to unlimited liability for the breaching party. It can even open the door to liability for consequential loss. So the invisible terms need to be noted among the high-risk terms.

MOST FREQUENT SOURCES OF CLAIMS AND DISPUTES

One way to recognize risky terms and issues (and reduce the probability that things will go wrong) is to learn from previous experiences involving claims and disputes. In its tenth Annual Survey, *2011 Top Terms in Negotiation,*[1] the International Association for Contract and Commercial Management (IACCM) asked negotiators—both sell-side and buy-side—from around the world what terms are considered the most frequent source of a claim or dispute. Table 5.1 summarizes the core findings:

The results show that delivery and acceptance issues constitute the most frequent source of claims and disputes. Experience tells us that this is probably due to confusion about requirements, either through ambiguity from the beginning or through the implementation (or lack) of change management procedures (number 3 on the list).

There is a major difference between these results and those listed among IACCM Top Terms of Today describing where negotiators spend most of their time in negotiating deals today. In the latter, year after year, terms such as liability limitations and indemnities top the list.[2] On the other hand, the IACCM Top Terms of the Future indicate that negotiators see more value in negotiating terms relating to change management, scope and goals, and the parties' responsibilities. The survey results present an opportunity to shift the focus of contract

---

1   IACCM (2011a) *2011 Top Terms in Negotiation.* International Association for Contract and Commercial Management, available at https://www.iaccm.com/members/library/files/top_terms_2011_1.pdf. See also Chapter 3 of this volume, Table 3.1.
2   See the left-hand column "Top Terms of Today" in Table 3.1 in Chapter 3 of this volume.

negotiation. Chapter 4 examined negotiation strategies and mindsets that can help make this shift happen, and Chapter 6 will introduce further ways in which mindsets and ways of working can be changed to enable a new focus, better decisions, and better results.

Table 5.1   IACCM 2011 most frequent sources of claims and disputes

Issue	% reported
Delivery/acceptance	41
Price/charge/price changes	38
Change management	32
Invoices/late payment	30
Performance/guarantees/undertakings	27
Service levels and warranties	27
Payment	25
Responsibilities of the parties	22
Liquidated damages	22
Scope and goals	21
Warranty	16
Limitation of liability	16
Indemnification	14
Service withdrawal or termination	14
Intellectual property	12
Audits/benchmarking	10
Assignment/transfer	8
Dispute resolution	8
Data protection/security	7
Communications and reporting	7

ACTIVE CLAUSES VS. PASSIVE CLAUSES— PERFORMANCE CONCERNS VS. LEGAL CONCERNS

One perspective on contract clauses is to view them as either "active" or "passive." This distinction, introduced by the IACCM,[3] is based on whether the term requires resources or action, or whether it comes into effect only if something happens or fails to happen. Active clauses are about *performance*: actions and roles that need to be performed to make things happen. They create obligations that need to be fulfilled. For example, payment terms and delivery terms are "active": they create specific obligations that require resources and supporting actions. Passive clauses, in turn, normally only enter the picture if those obligations are not fulfilled— for instance, if performance does not happen at all, in the right way, or at the right time. Passive clauses address issues such as liabilities, remedies, and force majeure.

Another distinction useful for our purposes is that made by law professors Ian Macneil and Paul Gudel. They divide *contract planning* into two main dimensions, *performance planning* and *risk planning*.[4] The first dimension is about the substance of the relationship, seeking to secure smooth and efficient performance and accomplishment of the parties' goals. The second dimension is about risk and contingencies: contract terms dealing with remedies, limitations of liability, indemnities, dispute resolution, and the like.

---

3   See, for instance, IACCM (2011b) *Contract and Commercial Management. The Operational Guide*. Zaltbommel: Van Haren Publishing, pp. 123, 366, 522.
4   Macneil, I.R. and Gudel, P.J. (2001) *Contracts—Exchange Transactions and Relations. Cases and Materials*, 3rd edn. New York, NY: Foundation Press.

Using the above approaches, it is easy to see how active clauses and passive clauses as well as performance planning and risk planning have an impact on contract risks and their management. However, conventional thinking about contract risk management tends to focus on passive clauses and risk planning. If something goes wrong, passive clauses are expected to work to the benefit of the party using them. However, this is *risk allocation*, not *risk management*!

Active clauses and performance planning should not be isolated from passive clauses and risk planning. While the former seem to fall into the domain of business and project managers and the latter into the domain of legal and risk management professionals, they are all intertwined, and their use should be synchronized. Otherwise, there is a real danger that, echoing Stewart Macaulay, there is a huge gap between the contract as written ("the paper deal") and the true agreement ("the real deal").[5]

When dealing with risk, it is important to see the difference between *causes* and *consequences* and address both. Passive clauses tend to deal mainly with the consequences of risk. While dealing with these consequences is important, businesses need to deal with causes and likelihood as well. This is where the active clauses play a key role. They should establish the foundation for a successful deal and relationship based on how the parties actually want to work together. Passive clauses, when used proactively, can help guide the relationship back on track when disturbances occur. They can help resolve disputes and minimize losses. What they cannot

---

5   Macaulay, S. (2003) The real and the paper deal: empirical pictures of relationships, complexity and the urge for transparent simple rules. In D. Campbell, H. Collins and J. Wightman (Eds.), *Implicit Dimension of Contracts: Discrete, Rational and Network Contracts*. Oxford: Hart Publishing, pp. 51–102, 51.

do is protect against bad judgment, bad business deals, or bad investments. Proper pre-contract planning—making sure the active clauses reflect the parties' true goals, needs, and expectations, and that the contract provides clarity about them—is indispensible.

Once active and passive clauses are agreed, they need to be followed. The resources required to meet obligations need to be available, and the agreed actions need to be taken at the right time and in the right way. For this to happen, both parties need to fully understand the operational aspects of the contract. The required obligations and actions must be understood by delivery teams and business and project managers responsible for implementation. When implementation succeeds and no unexpected events occur, there is normally no need to invoke the passive clauses. Making sure contractual promises are kept and obligations are fulfilled is one of the best ways to control contract risk.

HIGH-RISK ISSUES IN CONTRACTS

Some high-risk issues are frequently encountered in contracts across different deals and industries. In this section, we discuss examples of such issues on a general level. In a later section, we cover examples of risky contract clauses.

SCOPE AND PERFORMANCE: WHAT THE CONTRACT IS ABOUT AND WHAT IS IN AND OUT OF SCOPE

A basic—yet often neglected—question in connection with contract risk planning is: What is the scope of the contract? While seemingly self-evident, often it is not, and misunderstandings easily occur that can create a major contract risk for the supplier and the buyer alike. If the scope, specifications, or requirements are unclear, everything is unclear. The risk for the buyer is having to live with and pay for something that is not desired, while the risks for the supplier include not getting paid, and exposure to claims for damages, and perhaps cancellation. Both sides face the risk of engaging in a bitter, time-consuming and expensive dispute.

As stated in Chapter 2, disputes usually arise when someone has a sense of injury. This often results from a disappointed expectation. Some (but not all) of the expectations in a transaction or relationship are created by contractual provisions that describe what a party can or must do.[6]

Managing expectations is crucial, and requires communication. For the supplier, this entails finding out what the customer wants, guiding the customer to want what the supplier can provide, and clarifying what can be done within the framework of the proposed contract. Sometimes it is about making sure both parties are aware of the delivery limits and what will not be provided—that is, what is in and what is out of scope. Communication and clarity about scope, specifications and requirements promote shared expectations and reduce the possibility that one party's acts or failures to act will cause a disappointment for the other. In Chapter 6, we return to the issue of expectations, which are often invisible, and introduce *visualization* as a way to clarify and manage expectations and *make the invisible visible.*

---

6   See, generally, Dauer, E.A. (2006) The role of culture in legal risk management. In P. Wahlgren and C. Magnusson Sjöberg (Eds.), *A Proactive Approach. Scandinavian Studies in Law*, Volume 49. Stockholm: Stockholm Institute for Scandinavian Law, pp. 93–108, 95, available at http://www.scandinavianlaw.se/pdf/49-6.pdf.

WHO IS RESPONSIBLE FOR OUTCOMES? RESULTS OR RESOURCES?

An issue closely related to contract scope and performance is *responsibility*. Relationships are increasingly based on the delivery of outputs or outcomes. With the trend towards services and solutions comes increased supplier responsibility for performance, something that suppliers are not always aware of or willing to accept.

One of the basic questions in today's technology deals and contracts for services and solutions is whether what is purchased and sold and what will be provided constitute *results* or *resources*. This basic question is not as easy as it seems. Not all contracts—or requests for proposals or quotations, for that matter—are clear on this issue. Yet the question should be answered *before* making a commitment to sell or purchase, as the answer will often determine which party will bear responsibility for the results the buyer is expecting. At the same time, it will normally also determine who bears the risk of the negative consequences of not reaching those results.

So whose responsibility is it to produce the results? In broad terms, in a *results contract*, the supplier is responsible, while in a *resources contract*, the buyer is responsible. In many contracts, however, the nature and requirements of the contract in this regard are unclear. This can cause major business and legal problems.

In a clear-cut results contract, the supplier accepts the responsibility for and commits to certain results and thereby accepts the risk of failing to produce the results. The results may be expressed in terms of solutions, service levels, or outcomes. A true results contract drafted to protect the buyer does not trigger the buyer's obligation to pay until the supplier has produced the agreed results, either by reaching certain milestones or upon project completion. In the words of Joe Auer, President of International Computer Negotiations Inc., looking at the situation from the buyer's point of view, "there's nothing better than having a good contract—except having the vendor's money."[7]

Not all situations call for results-based contracts. Not all suppliers are prepared to accept and not all buyers propose such contracts. Risk versus price is one of the reasons. Sometimes results cannot be defined. Maybe the buyer just needs a piece of equipment and is prepared to take care of installation, commissioning, and everything else. Or maybe the buyer only needs advisory services or access to resources, such as maintenance technicians. Applying those resources and achieving the desired results is then the buyer's responsibility. In such cases, the parties may agree that a calendar date, product or service delivery, or the supplier's invoice can trigger the buyer's obligation to pay. A conventional contract based on *time and materials*—a resource contract—can work well for both suppliers and buyers in such cases, as long as the buyer does not expect the supplier to produce the final results or outcomes at a set price.

Because the question of responsibility for results is so important, a contract should provide a clear answer that reflects the parties' real needs and expectations. The answer should be clear, even though it is not always easy to contractually define the results or how they will be measured.

---

7   *Ten Truths of Negotiations—Truth #3 & #4*. Driving the Deal by ICN Blog hosted by Joe Auer, August 10, 2010, available at http://dobetterdeals.wordpress.com/tag/results-or-resources/.

In many contracts, responsibility becomes blurred when the contract leaves important issues to be decided later or states that the parties will accomplish something jointly. Who is then responsible? If the important question of responsibility for results is unclear, both parties are likely to suffer during performance. If a dispute arises, its outcome will be hard to predict. Proactive planning, careful communication, a true shared understanding, and a well thought-out contract that reflects the choices made can provide the answer.

GAPS IN CONTRACTS—ROOM FOR MISUNDERSTANDINGS AND UNINTENDED LIABILITIES?

As noted earlier, gaps in contracts (silence, lack of express terms) may be risky. What is *left out* of a contract— knowingly or unknowingly—can be at least as important as what is included. Gaps or omissions in contracts—what the contract does *not* say—leave room for invisible terms, which in turn can lead to unexpected results. Some contract gaps and omissions may be intentional, but many are not. While sometimes the parties deliberately choose to leave an issue unaddressed, often this is not the case. Instead, one or both of the parties may be unaware of the gap and its potential impact. When silence is used creatively[8] and both parties understand the impact, there might not be a problem. But unintended risk might result when the parties do not understand the implications of the silence created by those gaps and omissions.

---

8   Haapio, H. (2009) Invisible terms & creative silence: what you don't see can help or hurt you. *Contract Management*, September, 24–35, available at http://www.ncmahq. org/files/Articles/CM0909%20-%2024-35.pdf; and Haapio, H. (2004) Invisible terms in international contracts and what to do about them. *Contract Management*, July, 32–5, available at http://www.ncmahq.org/files/Articles/81EEB_cm_July04_32.pdf.

Some people care about text and clarity more than others. Lawyers typically care a lot. As illustrated by Figure 5.1, lawyers tend to see gaps even where most people see text that covers everything necessary.

Contract provisions are sometimes confusing, ambiguous, or vague. Because some terms, such as "bi-monthly" and "delivery," are easily misunderstood, they should be substituted with a better choice of words. In many cases, it does not take a lot of effort or require legal knowledge to prevent misunderstanding and express the intention of the parties more clearly.[9]

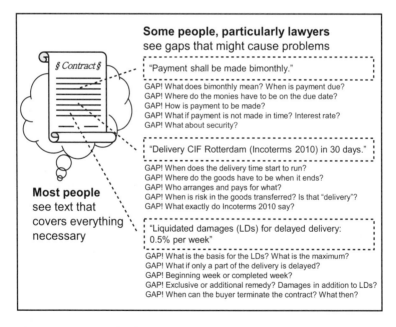

Figure 5.1   Mind the gaps in contracts!

---

9   For examples, see Haapio 2009 and 2004.

Some gaps are riskier than others. Unnecessary gaps and misunderstanding should be detected and prevented. In the following section, we show how the law can provide requirements where the parties have not been sufficiently clear as to what is required. While there is no substitute for contract clarity about performance and *active* clauses stipulating what needs to be done, by whom, and when, clarity about *passive* clauses is equally important. We cover unintended unlimited liability through gaps filled by invisible terms in a later section under the heading "Clauses that May be Risky—or Offer Protection against Risks."

UNSPECIFIED REQUIREMENTS—WHO NEEDS TO WORRY?

In the sale of consumer goods, where the seller is a business and the buyer is a consumer, consumer protection laws typically require that the goods conform to the requirements set by local law (unless the buyer intends to use the goods for a purpose where the requirement is of no significance). If the goods do not conform, they are considered to be defective. But business-to-business contracts might be different.

Consider a supplier outside the European Union selling machinery to a business buyer in an EU country. Let us assume that the contract specifications do not state what safety standards or requirements are to be followed and that those standards and requirements are different in the seller's country and in the buyer's country. In the country of the buyer, the requirements are mandatory: the machinery must satisfy EU health and safety requirements and national safety at work regulations. If the machinery fails to comply, the authorities can prohibit its use and, if the machinery was intended for resale, force it to be taken off the market. In addition, the party in breach may also be fined or even imprisoned. Must the seller know (or find out) about and comply with these unspecified requirements?[10]

The answer is the typical lawyer's answer: it depends. As between the seller and the buyer, the answer depends on the contract and the applicable law. Here, what the parties have agreed is always the starting point. If the contract is silent as to the safety, marking and other requirements, as in our case, then we need to look into the law applicable to the contract. In a legal assessment, the question is: If the goods sold by a business to a business do not conform with local legal requirements, are the goods defective? Can the buyer refuse to pay, cancel the contract, and claim damages? If the contract is silent and a dispute arises, it may take a long time to find the answers.

Buyers who think that it is self-evident that their country's mandatory product requirements need to be followed even in cross-border trade, even if not specified, may be in for a surprise. According to court rulings and legal literature, the general rule under the Convention on Contracts for the International Sale of Goods (CISG) is: unless expressly otherwise agreed, the seller cannot be expected to be aware of unspecified local requirements in the country of destination.

The goods do not necessarily need to comply with even *mandatory* requirements in the country of destination. However, there are exceptions to the rule, which may lead to the seller being expected to know or find out about and comply with unspecified local requirements. Examples

---

10   These may concern, for instance, requirements related to CE marking. CE is the abbreviation of "Conformité Européenne," French for "European Conformity." The party affixing CE marking indicates that the product is in conformity with the applicable requirements set out in Community harmonization legislation. Before the marking can be affixed, a number of complex technical requirements must be fulfilled.

include situations in which (1) the same requirements exist in the seller's country as well, (2) the buyer has pointed out the requirements to the seller and has relied and was entitled to rely on the seller's expertise, or (3) the seller knows—or the buyer can assume that the seller knows—the requirements "due to the particular circumstances of the case." Particular circumstances include contracts where the seller has a branch in the country of destination, the seller has had a business connection with the buyer for some time, or the seller often exports into the country in question.[11]

So who needs to worry in case of unspecified requirements? This example shows that unspecified requirements that might apply are a problem for *everyone* involved: the buyer, the seller, and the entire supply chain. They are a problem for requirement engineers, designers, project managers, field engineers, and people in charge of cost and margin. They may develop into a legal problem and dispute. Even if they do not, they present a frequently encountered technical and business problem: How can the seller fulfill (or pass on to its suppliers) requirements of which it is not aware?

If the requirements are not taken into account early enough, rework, delays and additional costs may result before the machinery is considered safe and can be used. Who is responsible for the rework and delays? Wrong question! Instead of asking questions about the consequences, the focus should be on the causes and *provide clarity* through specific, mutually understood requirements. The cause of the risk can be prevented from happening through cross-

---

11   The principles have been developed and affirmed by case law in different CISG member states. See, for instance, Unilex on CISG. Cases by Article & Issues, Article # 35, Issue 1.5, Conformity to public or other law requirements in buyer's country, available at http://www.unilex.info/dynasite.cfm?dssid=2376&dsmid=13356&x=35.

professional collaboration, proper planning, well thought-out requirements recognition and management, and careful contracting at the front end! Experienced manufacturers can help their suppliers and subs to comply, for instance, by providing training and easy-to-read guidance on safety-related and other requirements.

IS A CONTRACT OR CLAUSE LEGALLY BINDING AND ENFORCEABLE?

As we have seen in the previous chapters, contract law seeks to protect the parties' objectives by giving agreements legally binding force. Sometimes, however, one of the parties (or both) may see the law as interfering with the objectives—especially when a legal dispute arises. One of the questions that may arise then is whether a commitment is legally binding.

The parties do not always want to make legally binding commitments. Sometimes the parties want only one party to be legally committed, while the other remains not bound. Here we are not talking about so-called gentlemen's agreement, described by Didier Rigault as "an arrangement, which is not an agreement, between two persons, neither of whom is a gentleman, with each expecting the other to be strictly bound, while he himself has no intention of being bound at all."[12] Rather, we are thinking in terms of deliberately one-sided commitments, such as option contracts, where one party is committed and the other party has the right to choose whether it will exercise the option or not. Sometimes the situation necessitates postponing commitment for one party or both, or making commitment subject to certain conditions, such as obtaining financing or some approval or license.

---

12   Rigault, D. (1991) *Export Contracts. A Practical Guide*, 3rd edn. Oslo: Norwegian Trade Council, p. 15.

The parties' freedom of contract allows them to choose whether, when and to whom they want to commit themselves. Sometimes committing too early or, worse still, unknowingly, constitutes a major risk. If a party is not aware of the legally binding nature of one-sided offers in certain countries, it may come as a surprise if it has not expressly stated the terms and conditions for its offer. Or if a party mistakenly believes that the offer it has received is a legally binding commitment and the offeror then cancels or changes its offer, again, a negative surprise can follow.

Another area where the legal system may cause unexpected consequences is the enforceability of liability limitations. While you can generally use clauses in your contract that limit or exclude your liability, these do not work in all cases. There are liabilities you cannot limit, and contract clauses that attempt to do so may be unenforceable. There are, for example, legal restrictions on limiting liability for death or personal injury and for your own gross negligence or willful misconduct. Under some countries' laws, there are additional restrictions if you attempt to limit your liability through the use of standard terms. Under some laws, there are also form requirements related to the enforceability of liability limitations. For instance, you may need to use conspicuous text or specific words to exclude or limit liability.

You do not want to commit before you are ready to. Nor do you want to be misled by clauses that you believe limit your liability when in fact they do not. Understanding that the requirements of legally binding and enforceable commitments and clauses vary from one legal system to another is a good starting point. When you encounter an unfamiliar legal system governing your contract, asking for the advice of legal counsel familiar with that system is probably your best choice.

Many of the challenges, albeit not all, can be resolved by using clear language stating what the parties want. In this way, the parties can create clarity about what is legally binding. They can specify, for instance, whether they are creating absolute obligations, conditional obligations, or only preliminary plans, estimates, or non-binding intentions. Expressly stating whether the parties want their document (or parts of it) to be legally binding is especially important in pre-contractual documents, such as letters of intent. In addition, contract literacy and an awareness of risky areas, such as specific form or language requirements, is needed.

CLAUSES THAT MAY BE RISKY—OR OFFER PROTECTION AGAINST RISKS

Suppliers' contract terms typically contain limitations of liabilities that seek to protect the supplier against the consequences of contract breach, such as late delivery or delivery of defective goods or services. Buyers' contract terms typically lack such limitations. Instead, buyers may seek unlimited liability for the supplier. But the supplier might not be willing to accept (or able to insure against) unlimited liability. The two extremes are quite far apart, and the parties' bargaining position does not always lead to an optimal solution for both. What appears as a source of *contract risk* for one party may seem to be desirable *contract risk management* (or *risk allocation*) for the other party. Still the parties on both sides can and should use contracts proactively as planning and decision making tools to safeguard that risks are taken knowingly, balanced with reward, and managed. Here, the key word is *knowingly*.

The parties trying to allocate or transfer all risk to the other side need to remember that doing so does not make the risk disappear. The risk still exists and needs to be recognized and responded to, as its materialization usually has a negative impact on both parties and their relationship. It is better for both if the party in charge of the risk has taken the risk *knowingly* and is prepared to take the measures that are necessary to respond to it.

The following sections will list, with examples, a few of the most typical contract clauses, *visible terms*, that the parties should understand. In addition, we will continue the discussion of *invisible terms* (*lack of clauses*—gaps or silence) that might be filled in ways that are not what either party (or both) expected. In Chapter 6, we will cover possible ways to deal with risky clauses, whether visible or invisible.

UNLIMITED LIABILITY (THROUGH VISIBLE OR INVISIBLE TERMS)

Liability limits and unlimited liability cause constant friction between negotiating parties. Suppliers and buyers tend to address liability negotiation very differently, despite the fact that most businesses act as both suppliers and buyers. Although many contract and legal professionals understand the arguments for both sides very well, limitation of liability continues to be the most negotiated term on the list of IACCM Top Terms Today.

Unlimited liability through express contract terms is like a contractible or epidemic disease that begins when a buyer requires its suppliers to accept unlimited liability. (Some public organizations, for instance, have unlimited liability as part of their standard terms.) The prime or main contractors saddled with such contracts then want to push these terms down to their suppliers (and sometimes the law requires them to do so). The suppliers with these terms in turn seek similar undertakings from their suppliers, and so on. This easily leads to a contractual risk allocation that creates an illusion of control where none exists, as discussed in Chapter 3.

The problem with unlimited liability is that its extent is generally not predictable or controllable by the party accepting it. If it follows from a breach of contract, its limit may be the entire amount of the loss the other party suffers due to the breach. So the liability is basically what the name says: unlimited or limitless.

A buyer's insistence on the supplier's unlimited liability can lead to a higher price covering the risk, extended negotiation time, and a strained relationship. If the supplier accepts unlimited liability, the value of such a clause varies. Is the supplier capable of fulfilling it? Trying to enforce such a clause may lead to a long and expensive dispute, and a court judgment may not be easily enforceable. Even if it is, the supplier who has no assets might be uncollectible. Unlimited liability is generally not insurable, either.

Few businesses are willing to accept unlimited liability knowingly—yet sometimes they do so *unknowingly*. It is rather easy to spot a clause mentioning unlimited liability—much easier than to notice the *lack of limitation of liability*, which may in essence mean the same thing. The reason: *invisible terms*.

As noted earlier, most countries' default rules contain provisions stating that if a party breaches its contractual obligations and this leads to a loss suffered by the other party, then the latter party is entitled to *full compensation* for its loss. Depending on the applicable law and the situation at hand, this may include not only the loss which it suffered but also any gain of which it was deprived due to the breach. For instance, Article 74 of the CISG (on international sales of goods) states that "Damages for breach of contract by one party consist of a sum *equal to the loss, including loss of profit*, suffered by the other party as a consequence of the breach" (emphasis added). While laws contain certain conditions and requirements, such as the foreseeability of the loss at the time the contract was made, these seldom offer enough protection for the party in breach attempting to understand the extent of its liabilities. This is why most businesses will not (knowingly) accept unlimited liability. Instead, they require exclusion or some sort of limitation of liability in all of their contracts.

Let us take the example of a short sales contract (or a handshake deal) with no provisions dealing with liability. Does this mean that if the supplier is late or the goods fail and the buyer suffers a loss as a consequence, the supplier has no liability? Or is the buyer entitled to compensation for its loss, including loss of profit?

Obviously, the answer depends on *why* the delivery was late or *why* the goods failed, the chain of events, and questions such as whether the buyer caused or contributed to the delay and mitigated its loss and whether and when the buyer examined the goods and gave notice of the defect. Assuming that the buyer did what it was supposed to do and the seller was responsible for late delivery or failure of the goods to conform to the contract—and that this was the sole cause of the buyer's loss, the amount of which is proven—where do the parties stand?

As noted earlier, when the contract is silent, *invisible terms* (also known as gap-filling laws and default rules) enter the picture. The applicable law, such as the CISG, can supply terms that the parties might not know about. One common general principle of many gap-filling laws is the principle of *full compensation*: if you breach your contract, you have to compensate the other party for the loss it suffers due to the breach. While the conditions and wordings in various sales laws differ, they tend to protect the injured party—in this case, the buyer. The supplier may end up paying the buyer full compensation for its loss, including loss of profit.

The parties are free to opt out of default rules. Remaining silent is an option, but often not a very wise one. As we saw, silence leaves room for *invisible terms*. If a contract is breached, the law does not limit the breaching party's liability. Contracts do limit liability where the parties so provide. The damages when liability is not limited by contract—especially for consequential losses—can be astronomical, as the purchase price (or a percentage of it) does not automatically set a cap for the supplier's liability.

As illustrated by this discussion of unlimited liability, to properly recognize and deal with risk, a contract must be read not only for what it says, but also for what it does *not* say but perhaps should, the latter being often the more demanding task. In order to avoid negative surprises, gaps should be detected and addressed *before* they develop into business and legal problems. This is an area where contract literacy and liability disclaimers in the form of exclusion or limitation clauses come to the fore.

CLAUSES EXCLUDING OR LIMITING LIABILITY

Excluding or limiting liability is a central issue in many contract negotiations and disputes. Exclusion clauses—

clauses excluding liability for breach of contract—are typical
risk allocation tools that are frequently included in contracts
between businesses. Their contents differ. They may exclude
liability altogether, or liability for certain losses (for example,
consequential losses). They may also exclude certain remedies.
Typical examples of exclusion or limitation clauses include
the following:

- limitation of aggregate liability for damages to a specific
  amount or a percentage of the price

- disclaimers of liability for consequential loss

- limitation of liability to negligent acts or omissions only

- disclaimers and limitations related to seller's obligations
  and buyer's remedies for breach, such as delay in delivery
  or non-conformity

A limitation of liability clause often restricts the amount of
damages a party can recover from the other party. One of the
most common ways to do this is to set a liability cap. In some
contract types and industries, a percentage of the purchase
price or fee may be customary, in others, a multiple of the
price or fee. Here is a sample clause where the purchase price
is agreed to be the maximum of the supplier's liability:

*The Supplier's total liability in respect of any and
all claims for damages or losses, caused by breach
of contract, warranty, indemnity, tort (including
negligence), strict liability, statutory duty, or otherwise,
which may arise in connection with its performance or
non-performance under this contract, shall not exceed
in the aggregate the total purchase price.*

Normal profit margins charged to customers do not enable sellers to cover unlimited liability. The margin on the price typically bears no relation to the buyer's possible loss of revenue if the products are defective or if their delivery is delayed. Even where the products supplied are components used in the assembly of complex machinery or a production line, delay or defects may cause the buyer increased production costs or put the buyer in breach of large supply contracts with damages out of proportion to the price of the product supplied.

There are limitations on a seller's ability to limit liability. In consumer contracts, clauses that attempt to exclude or limit liability are often invalid. Even in contracts between businesses, some exclusion clauses might be invalid. Not all exclusion clauses become part of the contract, either. For instance, exclusion clauses that are included in standard terms and conditions (STCs) may have been sent to the other party too late to become part of the contract. Some countries' laws (for instance, in Germany and England) have requirements and limitations for such clauses when part of STCs. In some countries, the law may disregard the exclusion clause (whether in individual or in standard terms) if it is unfair or unreasonable—for example, an attempted exclusion of liability for death or personal injury. The same is true for attempts to exclude (or limit) liability for grossly negligent or intentional breaches.

CLAUSES DEALING WITH CONSEQUENTIAL LOSS

There are two different situations where liability for consequential losses may arise: either by express terms (specific undertakings in the contract) or by implied terms (default rules). The latter are harder to recognize, as they cannot be detected by simply reading the contract. They are "invisible terms." Because accepting liability for such losses involves the acceptance of risks that are hard to assess, consequential losses are customarily excluded from contractual liability.

The simplest limitation of liability clause addressing consequential loss may state: "In no event shall the parties be liable for any consequential loss." or "In no event shall the Supplier be liable to the Purchaser for any consequential loss." But what do these clauses actually mean? While there is a general understanding that you should usually attempt to exclude liability for consequential loss, there is no universal, global truth as to what "consequential loss" means.

In some countries and situations, loss of profits is consequential loss; in others it is not. Laws differ considerably. The CISG, for example, does not mention consequential loss. Instead, it states that all foreseeable losses caused by the breach, including loss of profit, need to be compensated. It is therefore safest to "make your own law" through your contract and clarify what kinds of losses you want to exclude.

To provide more clarity about consequential loss, many limitation clauses list the damages and losses that are excluded—for example, "loss of revenue, loss of profit, loss of contract, loss of business, loss of use, loss of production, interruption of business, loss of operation time, costs of capital, cost in connection with interruption of operation, economic loss," with the addition "or any special, incidental or consequential loss or damage howsoever caused." A non-exhaustive list of examples is typically part of a supplier's contract terms. A buyer would typically want a shorter list. In addition to a clause excluding liability for consequential loss, a supplier would normally want to have a monetary cap for damages relative to the purchase price.

LIQUIDATED DAMAGES AND OTHER AGREED REMEDIES CLAUSES

If a delivery is late and the buyer suffers a loss as a consequence, the buyer is entitled to damages in accordance with the applicable law—unless the contract says otherwise. A buyer who claims damages might first have to expend time and money on litigation, the outcome of which may be difficult to predict. The buyer has to prove its loss and to do everything in its power to mitigate the loss. To avoid unnecessary trouble, *agreed remedies* such as liquidated damages can offer a better way.

Contracting parties in business-to-business dealings often amend the default rules—in particular the remedial rules— of the sales laws by using *liquidated damages clauses* in their contracts. Such clauses can be found in individually negotiated terms and in STCs. They are frequently used in connection with delivery and performance guarantees. Here is an example of a liquidated damages clause relating to a delay in delivery:

> *If the Product is not delivered at the time for delivery, the Purchaser is entitled to liquidated damages from the date on which delivery should have taken place. The liquidated damages shall be payable at a rate of 0.5 percent of the purchase price for each completed week of delay. The liquidated damages shall not exceed 7.5 percent of the purchase price.*

Because liquidated damages clauses vary, you need to be aware of *what kind* of liquidated damages you are dealing with. Whether a liquidated damages clause *limits* or *adds to* the supplier's liability for damages depends on the clause and on the applicable law, which determines how the clause is interpreted in case of a legal dispute. Not all clauses are enforceable as written.

Some contracts contain clauses providing that the buyer is entitled to *both* liquidated damages *and* damages for the entire loss it has suffered, while others provide liquidated damages and expressly state that these are the only remedy. The former (which can open the door to consequential loss claims) favor the buyer; the latter favor the supplier. Here is an example of the latter kind:

> *Liquidated damages (and termination of the contract with limited compensation as stated above) are the only remedies available to the Purchaser in case of delay on the part of the Supplier. All other claims against the Supplier based on such delay shall be excluded, except where the Supplier has been guilty of gross negligence.*

So liquidated damages can limit liability and remedies, or can provide for additional liability and remedies. Where the latter is the case, the default rules of the applicable law (invisible terms) have to be taken into account. While it is rather easy to spot a clause mentioning additional or cumulative remedies, it is more difficult to spot the lack of a clause stating that the agreed remedies are exclusive. The lack of such a clause may in fact lead to the same outcome: agreed remedies cumulated with remedies provided by the applicable law. Contract literacy requires that you understand both agreed and invisible terms, as illustrated in Figure 5.2.

Contracting parties generally use liquidated damages clauses to remove uncertainty and avoid litigation costs. However, in some circumstances, courts might still intervene. In some

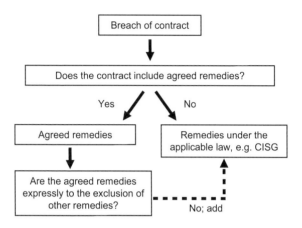

Figure 5.2   Applying   contract   literacy   to   agreed remedies

legal systems, for instance, the sum stipulated may be reduced by the courts if it is considered excessive or invalidated if the clause is considered a penalty. Common law systems generally distinguish between penalty clauses (which are not permitted) and liquidated damages clauses (which are permitted), the latter being based on a genuine estimate of the loss suffered as a result of the breach. Whether the parties call their clause a penalty or liquidated damages is not decisive. If a stipulated amount is to be paid in addition to the actual loss suffered, it may be considered invalid as a penalty.[13]

To provide clarity, you should state whether the liquidated damages clause excludes or is in addition to other remedies

---

13   For the application of liquidated damages clauses and other boilerplate clauses under English law as opposed to German, French, Italian, Danish, Finnish, Norwegian, Swedish, Hungarian, and Russian law, see Cordero-Moss, G. (Ed.) (2011) *Boilerplate Clauses, International Commercial Contracts and the Applicable Law*. Cambridge: Cambridge University Press. The parties will likely choose the governing law of their agreement on the basis of whether their agreement will be upheld under that law.

and make sure that you understand its impact. To control risks, your organization needs to have a basic understanding of both contracts (including STCs, where involved) and the applicable laws. They need *contract literacy*.

Depending on their contents, liquidated damages and other agreed remedies clauses may be pro-supplier or pro-buyer. The following table lists examples of both.

Table 5.2   Examples of agreed remedies, pro-supplier and pro-buyer

Pro-supplier:
• Promise *only* liquidated damages in case of delay in delivery
• Promise *only* to repair or replace if the goods are defective
• Agreed remedies specified to be *exclusive remedies:* no room for default rules/invisible terms.

Pro-buyer:
• High liquidated damages payable irrespective of buyer's actual loss
• Right to reject goods that fail to conform "in any respect"
• Agreed remedies specified to be *additional remedies;* remedies based on default rules/invisible terms also apply.

When used to specify limitation of liability and remedies, contract clauses can provide protection for a party who breaches the contract. Clauses that contain additional liabilities and remedies protect the innocent party. Both types of clauses are used as contractual tools for allocating risk. Ideally, their content and impact are understood *before* accepting them. But they do not protect the parties using them from liability to third parties who have not signed the contract. This is where indemnities and hold harmless clauses enter the picture.

INDEMNITIES OR HOLD HARMLESS CLAUSES

Year after year, indemnities have been among the top three of IACCM Top Terms Today. They are frequently encountered in business negotiations and contracts, especially when dealing with businesses in countries or industries following Anglo-American contracting practices. These businesses often propose indemnity and hold harmless clauses under which they seek to transfer or limit their liability. In the Nordic and Central European countries, these clauses are relatively new "legal transplants" still lacking an established translation.

An indemnity often includes a commitment to compensate the other party who is liable if a third party presents a claim—for instance if the supplied goods cause damage to third-party property or infringe a third party's intellectual property rights. The basic idea is that the supplier will pay to the buyer what the buyer has to pay to the third party. In addition, an indemnity may provide that the supplier shall take care of the relevant investigations, litigation, and defense, along with related expenses. Such a promise can cause a heavy financial burden and represent a major source of contract risk. Like any other clauses, indemnity clauses are interpreted according to their content. When accepting an indemnity, the indemnitor (the party giving the indemnity) accepts the risk that the indemnitee (the party to whom the indemnity is given) will make a claim for payment under the indemnity. The contents of indemnity clauses must therefore be studied carefully before accepting them.

Indemnity clauses come in many shapes and forms. The purpose of the clause may be to transfer liability—for instance, where the indemnitee is exposed to liability to third parties, or reverse liability. Sometimes indemnity clauses reinforce liability that would arise anyway. Here is one example:

> *The Contractor agrees to indemnify the Purchaser against loss or damage to any property and claims by any person against the Purchaser in respect of bodily injury or death arising out of or as a consequence of the sole negligence of the Contractor in the performance of this Contract.*

Here is another example:

> *The Contractor agrees to indemnify the Purchaser against any and all loss or damage, personal injury or death (including any indirect or consequential loss) howsoever caused suffered by the Purchaser, its officers, servants, or agents, or anyone claiming through or against the Purchaser, arising during, out of or as a consequence of the performance of this Contract and whether caused by or contributed to by the Purchaser or others.*

While it is noteworthy that there is no monetary cap or time limit to either indemnity, the two examples are quite different. The first indemnity clause covers property damage and personal injury or death caused by the contractor's sole negligence in the performance of the contract. The second indemnity clause is much broader, almost limitless, and includes indirect and consequential loss. The second clause might add to the contractor's liability under local law. Liability based on such a clause alone would not be covered under customary liability insurance and it might prove expensive, if not impossible, to obtain special insurance to cover such liability.

Some indemnity clauses may be so unevenly balanced in favor of one party that they are considered unenforceable. There are specific anti-indemnity statutes and limits to what courts will enforce in some contexts and countries. Yet one should not take indemnities lightly. The basic assumption between businesses remains that if a clause, indemnity or otherwise, has been made part of the contract, it has been accepted and understood.

So you should read clauses carefully before committing to them. In business-to-business dealings, where freedom of contract prevails, you want to make sure that you understand what the proposed indemnity clause entails, what can trigger liability under the clause, how far liability may extend, and how long it may last. The answers depend on the language of the indemnity clause and the context in which the clause is used.

One of the dangers for the indemnitor (and often one of the main goals of the indemnitee) is that indemnity clauses might set aside the limitations of liability that would otherwise protect the indemnifying party. Unless a supplier-indemnitor pays attention, the indemnity may unintentionally compromise a limitation of liability that was intended to cap the supplier's liability to a percentage of the purchase price or exclude consequential damages from the scope of the supplier's liability. As an indemnitor, you want the limitations to apply to the indemnity clause as well, and to clarify that the total aggregate maximum liability covers any liability under the indemnity.

It is also necessary to coordinate the contents of the indemnity clause with the coverage of your liability insurance, which may not cover your indemnity-based obligations and responsibilities. If the standard insurance policy limits coverage for bodily injury and property damage to negligence (tort liability) or legal (statutory) liability only, you should acquire additional coverage.

Indemnity clauses are sometimes compared to liability and legal expenses insurance. The purpose is to transfer to the indemnitor the ultimate financial responsibility for the damage caused. If you as the indemnitor are prepared to work as your indemnitee's "liability insurance carrier," keep in mind that you, like an insurance company, should set a maximum liability—and charge a premium.

Despite potential limitations, indemnity clauses can be valuable for the indemnitee in cases where one is exposed to liability to third parties, such as product liability or liability for intellectual property infringement. If you are requesting an indemnity from your contracting party, you need to use clear words and carefully review the wording, as courts tend to interpret such clauses against their drafter or user. And you need to remember that indemnity clauses are only as good as the indemnitor's ability to respond. If the indemnitor's financial resources are not strong and there is possible exposure to extensive liability, you should consider requiring the indemnity to be supported by a bank guarantee or other security. This, in turn, is likely to have an additional cost attached to it.

FURTHER EXAMPLES OF RISKY CLAUSES

Some contract clauses are copy-pasted from previous contracts and used repeatedly, without much attention to what they mean. This is especially true for clauses considered to be "part of the boilerplate." Not many business people read their own or the other side's boilerplate clauses. Someone, however, should pay attention to such clauses. We now turn to a few clauses that may prove to be quite risky.

A *time of the essence clause* can stand alone or be part of a clause dealing with performance. It may simply state: *Time is of the essence*. It may also state whose or what performance it relates to—for example: "The Supplier shall deliver the goods to the buyer's premises by [date], time being of the essence."

The concept of *time of the essence* is deeply rooted in some legal traditions and unknown in others, where the interpretation of the clause is somewhat uncertain. The clause might not be discussed during contract negotiations. Non-native speakers representing the sell-side may agree that foreign law governs the contract and accept the proposed clause without knowing that the ordinary-looking words *time is of the essence* carry a specific legal meaning. What the phrase actually means (under the legal systems where it is recognized) is that the performance in question is so essential that any breach amounts to a fundamental breach of the contract. A fundamental breach, in turn, normally entitles the non-breaching party to terminate the contract.

If the seller's negotiators knew that, they would probably not agree that *any* delay in delivery is a fundamental breach entitling the other party to terminate. They might rather work out a solution using a grace period and liquidated damages and build in more clarity as to when and how the contract can be terminated and what the consequences are.

While a risk management tool for a buyer whose plans change, a contract that contains a *termination for convenience* clause can be a high-risk contract for a contractor. Predictability is low when the continuation of the project depends solely on the other party. While the clauses and their compensation conditions differ, in most cases when the contract is terminated for convenience the contractor will lose money and seldom earn the profit that it anticipated when making the contract.

Termination for convenience clauses differ from termination for cause clauses in that they allow termination without any fault on the part of the contractor. The clause might read like this: "The Owner may at any time and for any reason terminate the Contractor's services and work at the Owner's convenience." The clause might also state: "Upon receipt of such notice, the Contractor shall immediately discontinue the work and placing of orders for materials, facilities and supplies." While such clauses are customary in certain projects and industries, they can (and should) be deal killers in others.

Some contractors use another type of risk-oriented clause, *pay-when-paid* or *pay-if-paid*, to pass the risk of not being paid down the chain to their subcontractors. A pay-when-paid clause can read, for example: "The Contractor shall pay the Subcontractor when the Contractor receives payment from the Owner." Or, taken from the standard form of a contractor: "Payments will be made not more than thirty (30) days from the submission date or ten (10) days from the certification or when we have been paid by the Owner, whichever is the later." A pay-if-paid clause might read, for example: "Payment by the Owner to the Contractor is a condition precedent to the Contractor paying the Subcontractor." Sometimes the clause continues by highlighting the risk to the subcontractor: "The Subcontractor understands and agrees that it will be paid if, and only after, the Contractor is paid by the Owner. The Subcontractor fully understands that it bears the risk of non-payment by the Owner."

Sometimes such clauses go unnoticed by subcontractors, who often have no way to control such risk. The reason for non-payment might be the contractor's default under its contract with the buyer, whose financial status the subcontractor may not know and may not be able to ascertain. The use of such clauses is not without risk for the contractor, either. Courts have differing views as to whether pay-when-paid clauses specify a condition governing the subcontractor's legal entitlement to payment or merely the time of payment. To be effective, the clauses must be worded clearly. Even then, laws in some countries prohibit such clauses or allow them in very limited circumstances. In any case, such clauses— unless read, fully understood and knowingly accepted—can create uncertainty and friction and increase the risk of matters ending up in a legal dispute.

Another clause that can be either risky or a valuable risk management tool is the *suspension of work* clause. Many contracts (and standard contract forms and terms) give the buyer the right to suspend work not only for cause but also for convenience. A *suspension of work* clause, when used as a risk management tool by the buyer, results in uncertainty and risk for the supplier, as the schedule, the dynamics of work and payment, are then out of its control. While the supplier might include the same clause in contracts with its own suppliers and subcontractors, the risk of not being paid still remains.

On the other hand, the supplier can use a *suspension of work* clause as a risk management tool for its protection in case the buyer does not pay. This situation becomes more risky to the supplier as the project moves forward. For example, as a construction project nears completion, the contractor loses—and the owner gains—leverage. Close to obtaining a completed project, the owner might be inclined to suspend or reduce payments to the contractor. If the contractor continues working regardless of non-payment and completes the project, the contractor loses whatever commercial leverage it had because the owner has already received what it needs.

If the contract contains a *suspension of work* clause, the unpaid supplier/contractor can suspend work. The clause might read, for instance: "If the Owner fails to pay the Contractor any amount due within 14 days from the due date, the Contractor may, after giving 7 days' prior notice to the Owner, suspend work." Without a clause specifying the procedure and timeline, the issue of whether and when non-payment becomes a material breach of contract justifying suspension (or termination) by the contractor is a gray area. The laws of different countries vary. A contractor who has not been paid and whose contract does not include a *suspension of work* clause might have to wait several weeks before suspending work. A contractor who suspends (or terminates) work too early risks breaching the contract, with all the consequences that can follow.

Choice of law and dispute resolution clauses might seem standard and of little, if any, business value. However, they can be pivotal to whether and how well a contract works as a risk management tool. There are many aspects to this, one being the *invisible terms* that are determined by the choice of law. If the parties do not choose law or dispute resolution forum, then the implied terms make that choice for them. As noted earlier, different countries have different requirements regarding, for example, the formation of a contract and what becomes part of it and regarding the validity of liability disclaimers and limitations.

Choice of law and dispute resolution clauses should provide clarity and legal predictability if a legal dispute arises. At this point, carefully made choices will prove valuable, as these clauses may literally make or break the contract.

Selecting the "wrong" applicable law or dispute resolution forum may be expensive and cumbersome and bring disastrous results. Your entire contract or your disclaimers or limitations may not be legally binding and you may lose the protection you thought that you had. Choosing your own country's court system as the exclusive dispute resolution forum may lead to losing even if you win because the other party may have no assets in your country and your winning court judgment may not be enforceable in the other party's country. While arbitral awards are widely enforceable globally, court judgments can be more difficult to enforce.

An *attorneys' fees clause* (or the lack of such a clause) is another area where contracts—especially when made across borders—may lead to a negative surprise. Many Europeans take it for granted that if you win a dispute you will automatically have the right to have your attorneys' fees compensated—that is, the loser pays. This, however, is not the general rule in the United States—unless your contract provides otherwise.

The above examples illustrate some typical high-risk issues and risky clauses in contracts. Many of them represent risk allocation or risk transfer clauses. A number of further examples could be added, such as on-demand bond or insurance requirements, force majeure clauses, and notice requirements. While many of them may seem desirable risk control mechanisms for one party, they can also represent a major risk. In reality, such clauses do not make the risk disappear. Instead, they may lead to risks being allocated to parties unable to manage them. In the long run, this is not in anyone's best interest. In Chapter 6, we will explore ways in which businesses can deal with risky issues and clauses and secure systematic contract risk recognition and response.

SUMMARY

This chapter discusses risky terms and issues in contracts. It examines contract risks that impact business objectives (performance, benefits) and those that impact legal objectives and illustrates that in many cases, these two types of risks are intertwined. To succeed in managing risky terms and issues in contracts and benefit from this chapter, you should:

1. Use contracts proactively as planning and decision making tools to safeguard that risks are taken knowingly, balanced with reward, and managed. Here, the key word is *knowingly*.

2. Remember that allocating or transferring the risk to the other side does not make the risk disappear. You still must identify and respond to the risk.

3. Make sure your organization recognizes that contract terms dealing with risk extend beyond those mentioning risk or addressing legal concerns and include clauses dealing with performance concerns. The right contract

structure and terms can make all the difference between success and failure and can play a key role in customer and supplier satisfaction.

4. Focus on high-risk issues, such as scope and performance and who is responsible for outcomes. Use your contract literacy to make sure there are no unrecognized risky terms or gaps that leave room for misunderstandings and unintended liabilities.

5. Be aware of the risks related to unlimited liability, whether created through visible (express) or invisible (implied) terms. Do not accept such liability or expect your contract partners to do so without appropriate balance with the reward.

6. Do not accept anything in the contract you do not fully understand. Even boilerplate provisions and the small print can have a major impact on the success of your company.

⑥ Contract Risk Recognition and Response: Processes and Tools

Contracts may seem complex at first, and some contracts truly are. Contracts are about business, and today's business is seldom simple. Adding risks and legal aspects to the picture does not make things easier. Yet sometimes attitudes and perceptions make things sound more complicated than they are or need to be.

Some businesses have dedicated contract professionals. In others, the "contract manager" might actually be a project manager, sales manager, procurement manager, an engineer, or a lawyer. During the contract's lifecycle, all of these functions may be involved in contract-related tasks. As noted in Chapter 1, ultimately the responsibility for business contracts and for the management of contract risks will fall on the shoulders of business leaders and executives.

Contract risk management can be implemented or improved in small steps that do not necessarily require major investments of time or resources. It can be embedded into the tasks that individuals carry out as part of their job. Tools and guidance can be provided that help them integrate contract risk management into their day-to-day work and enhance their skills.

This chapter begins with a discussion of the contract risk management process, including process vocabulary, frameworks, and a focus that incorporates the basic principles of risk management. The chapter then introduces a practical tool for implementing contract risk management: the four-step Contract Risk and Opportunity Management Plan, including specific examples, tools, and techniques. Ownership and accountability, key elements necessary for this—or any other—plan to succeed, are then covered.

Toward the end of this chapter, we illustrate why today's businesses need to manage risks *jointly*, moving from *risk allocation* to true *risk management*. One way of doing this is to build an early warning system and joint risk management into the contract. Engaging people and communicating contracts are especially important—and challenging—when managing contract risk. The chapter concludes by showing how visualization can be used to meet this challenge, including a lean and visual (IKEA) approach to contracts and contract risk management.

IMPLEMENTING CONTRACT RISK MANAGEMENT: NEITHER EXPENSIVE NOR COMPLICATED

Contract risk management does not have to be overly expensive or complicated. Today's businesses possess a wide range of contract-related and risk management-oriented skills and capabilities. Many business, project, and legal professionals already apply contract risk management steps successfully as part of their job. The challenge is educating new people to do the same and transforming the skills and knowledge of experienced individuals to organization-level competence.

The transfer of data, information and knowledge becomes particularly visible when people leave the organization and their contract-related responsibilities need to be reallocated. The more these individuals keep in their files, to-do lists, email inbox, personal task manager, or memory, the more difficult it will be for others to take over. Will all contracts still be fulfilled or monitored? And where are those contracts? Access to them must be secured to those who need to know, regardless of changes in personnel. Yet continuity does not happen by itself—it needs to be planned.

Contract risk management solutions vary depending on the size of the organization, the value and nature of its deals and relationships, and situation-specific issues. Some approaches are universal. Contract risk management can in many cases be built in into the activities, systems and processes that businesses already have in place—for example, within the framework of business excellence or quality management initiatives, enterprise risk management, corporate governance, contract management, or project management. It can be linked to existing procedures, such as bid and contract reviews, audits, and self-assessment activities. With some updating and refining, these processes can be adjusted to secure ongoing and systematic recognition of and response to contract risks and opportunities.

USING QUALITY PRINCIPLES TO IMPLEMENT CONTRACT RISK MANAGEMENT: A CASE STUDY

Philip Crosby, one of the leading philosophers of quality management, once noted:

> *Business consists of transactions and relationships. Quality management's purpose is to cause all transactions to be complete and correct, while all relationships are to be successful. If we understand those two sentences we know all we need to know about quality management.*[1]

In light of Crosby's profound truth, contract risk management and quality management have a lot in common. The following case study[2] shows how the latter can help improve the former. The work of the Better Agreement Team at Molzen-Corbin & Associates, an Albuquerque engineering and architectural firm, illustrates the benefits that are possible from a quality-oriented approach, a measurable goal, and scoring. It also demonstrates that you do not have to be a lawyer to improve the contracting process or the management of contract risks.

---

1   Crosby, P.B. (1996) *Quality Is Still Free. Making Quality Certain in Uncertain Times.* New York, NY: McGraw-Hill, p. 21.
2   The case study and quotations are from Clark, R.H. and Paul, R.A. (1996) Improving professional services agreements: a case history. In *ASQC 50th Annual Quality Congress Proceedings.* Milwaukee, WI: American Society for Quality Control, pp. 788–93.

At one time, Molzen-Corbin developed their professional services contracts the way many companies do: they used old contract forms—each project manager had their own—or they agreed to their clients' proposals for contracts. This approach continued until they realized that the profit from—and the risk assumed in—a project depended on the contract. The firm found that to remain viable, it had to negotiate equitable agreements that limit the risks assumed and allow an acceptable profit. Within the framework of a quality initiative that had been launched in the firm, a Better Agreement Team (BAT) was appointed to improve contracts and the contracting process. The team included three engineering project managers, the company's accountant, and the executive vice president. The chief executive officer gave full support to the effort.

The BAT developed a "what makes a perfect agreement" list and selected provisions that should be included in a "perfect" professional services agreement. A 1–page, 32-item checklist was developed with points assigned to each provision related to its relative importance. A "perfect" agreement would include all those provisions and score 100. Copies of recent agreements were scored by the BAT. The average score for them was 49, with a high of 79 and a low of 14. There was definitely room for improvement. The BAT analyzed the existing situation, located the fundamental reasons for "defects" in contracts, and prioritized the areas that needed improvement. Then they suggested three areas for improving the contracting process:

1. "Perfect" Agreement Forms: develop "perfect" draft agreements so that project managers could begin the preparation of a contract with an appropriate "perfect" form that would score 100,

2. Agreement Training and Reference Notebook: provide managers with training and a notebook that includes the provisions of a "perfect" contract (with background information as to their intent and importance) that they can use when preparing contracts, and

3. Agreement Checklist: before executing contracts, require a completed checklist in which a "yes" answer to all questions indicates a "perfect" contract and a "no" answer requires a "why not" explanation.

The firm's agreements did indeed improve. In a test conducted after a small group of project managers had followed the new process, the average score was 68—a major improvement compared to 49 for the earlier tested agreements. The test results encouraged the firm to implement BAT recommendations. Project managers and management were informed about the new process, and training was provided. In the next test after implementation, the average score of the contracts was 71. The BAT succeeded, and the results were measurable. Several additions to the "what makes a perfect agreement" list were identified during testing and implementation, and these provisions were incorporated into the forms, notebook, and checklist. The ongoing review of the "why not" responses allows identification of further opportunities to improve agreements.

In summary, Molzen-Corbin realized that contracts impact risk and that the management of contracts and risks can be improved using quality management methodologies. Contract risk management was improved by providing people in charge of the pre-contract process—in this case, the project managers—with easy access to common tools such as contract forms, notebooks, and checklists. As this example illustrates, development of the tools does not need to be complicated.

TOWARDS SYSTEMATIC CONTRACT RISK MANAGEMENT

To move towards more systematic contract risk management, a framework and vocabulary are necessary. Existing risk management standards are often confusing because *risk management* and the *risk management process* have been defined in different ways by different professional bodies and standards organizations. Some companies and industries have also developed their own language. As shown in the following three examples, the language used for the steps in the risk management process varies also.[3]

The ISO Risk Management Standard (ISO 31000:2009) defines risk management as "coordinated activities to direct and control an organization with regard to risk." The "coordinated activities" are achieved through a process, where the main steps are risk assessment—the overall process of risk identification, risk analysis, and risk evaluation—and risk treatment. At all steps, the process also involves communication and consultation along with monitoring and review.

The IRM/ALARM/AIRMIC Risk Management Standard sees risk management as "the process whereby organizations methodically address the risks attaching to their activities with the goal of achieving sustained benefit within each activity and across the portfolio of all activities." This Standard begins

---

3   For a comparison of risk management standards, see Table 2.1 in Pullan, P. and Murray-Webster, R. (2011) *A Short Guide to Facilitating Risk Management*. Farnham: Gower Publishing, pp. 11–13, with references.

the risk management process with the strategic objectives of the organization and includes in the process the steps of risk assessment (including risk analysis—that is, risk identification, risk description, and risk estimation), risk evaluation, risk reporting (threats and opportunities), risk treatment, residual risk reporting, and monitoring.

The *PMI Guide to the Project Management Body of Knowledge*, in turn, defines *project risk management* as a process that includes conducting risk management planning, risk identification, risk analysis, risk response planning, and monitoring and control.[4]

THE CONTRACT RISK MANAGEMENT PROCESS: RECOGNITION—REVIEW—RESPONSE

While the language of different standards and corporate processes vary, general agreement seems to exist about the focus of the risk management process: the recognition (identification) and treatment of risks, the latter being based on decisions following analysis. A well-developed risk management process helps those involved in contracting understand what is risky, assess the degree or level of risk, understand the consequences of particular events occurring, and develop actions to control the event or minimize its consequences.

Thus, the contract risk management process covers the following principal steps: (1) Risk recognition: identifying the potential sources of contract risk (threats), their causes and consequences; (2) risk review: estimating and prioritizing the risks based on their potential likelihood and impact; and (3)

---

4   *A Guide to the Project Management Body of Knowledge (PMBOK® Guide)* (2008) 4th edn. Newtown Square, PA: Project Management Institute (PMI), p. 273.

risk response: responding to risks that are considered most important. The contract risk management process and its principal steps are shown in Figure 6.1.

Like risk management in general, contract risk management is not a one-time event. While front-end risk mitigation is important, risk management is needed throughout the lifecycle of the contract. Here, the transition between the pre-contract, contract, and post-contract teams and possible gaps when accountability is transferred from one team to another require special attention. As illustrated in Figure 6.1, communication is crucial throughout the process, and contract risks require continuous monitoring.

Many tools and methodologies that help businesses recognize, review, and respond to risks are useful in the contracting process. These include checklists, guidance documents,

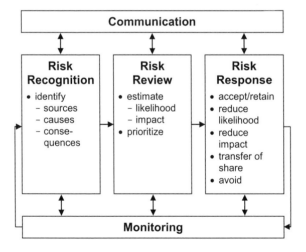

Figure 6.1 The contract risk management process

handbooks, questionnaires, and interactive software tools. In the field of health and safety, many tools can be downloaded for free. For example, the European Agency for Safety and Health at Work (EU-OSHA) has developed a risk assessment tools database.[5] Some tools are generic and others are industry, branch, or risk-specific.

Opportunities, like risks, are about uncertainties that may have an impact on the achievement of objectives. While the language varies, the same process and many of the same tools can also be applied to "upside risks"—opportunities. These, too, have sources (or drivers), likelihood, and impact (consequences, benefits) that need to be addressed.

THE BASIC PRINCIPLES OF RISK MANAGEMENT

Risk management should create and protect value.[6] The resources expended to mitigate risk should be less than the consequence of inaction. In other words, risk management should be cost effective.

To be properly managed, risk should be *allocated to the party best able to carry it*.[7] To be able to carry risk, the party in charge should be aware of the risk. Risk research on projects and supply chains has identified a number of further principles that should be followed by all participants in a project supply chain:[8]

---

5   http://osha.europa.eu/en/practical-solutions/risk-assessment-tools.
6   This is the first principle of risk management as stated in the ISO Risk Management Standard (ISO 31000:2009), p. 23.
7   See, for example, Mahler, T. (2010) Legal risk management—developing and evaluating elements of a method for proactive legal analyses, with a particular focus on contracts. Doctoral Thesis. Faculty of Law, Oslo: University of Oslo, p. 114, with references.
8   Loosemore, M., Raftery, J., Reilly, C. and Higgon, D. (2006) *Risk Management in Projects*, 2nd edn. Abingdon: Taylor & Francis, p. 161; see also Loosemore, M. and

---

Risks should only be taken by those who:

- have been made fully aware of the risks they are taking,
- have the necessary capacity (expertise and authority) to avoid, minimize, monitor, and control a risk,
- have the necessary resources to cope with the risk if it occurs,
- have the necessary risk attitude to want to take on the level of risk, and
- are able to charge an appropriate premium for taking on the risk.

The theory is that by following these principles, one can create a supply chain with a *common perception* of risk allocation and appropriately located incentives to manage the risks effectively. Not following these principles, on the other hand, can cause confusion about responsibility for risks and create the illusion of risk transfer.[9] This, in turn, can lead to early signals of problems going unnoticed, leading to delayed action. If the problem is allowed to grow, its prevention and control become more difficult and its consequences become more serious. This easily leads to disputes between the parties about who is to blame and where responsibility lies. In this way, wrong or unrealistic risk allocation can increase risk, rather than reduce it, and the escalated risk may default back to the party who thought that it had effectively freed itself and transferred the risk to others.[10]

McCarthy, C.S. (2008) Perceptions of contractual risk allocation in construction supply chains. *Journal of Professional Issues in Engineering Education and Practice*, 134(1), 95–105, p. 95.

9   Loosemore et al. 2006 and Loosemore and McCarthy 2008. See also Chapter 3.

10   Loosemore and McCarthy 2008, p. 95.

While these principles are easy to understand, they are not always easy to follow. What makes business sense and is desirable in business practice may not always be supported by legal rules or contract practice. For example, it is not a *legal* requirement that a party, in order to be obligated to bear certain contract risks, is fully aware of them. Nor is it a *legal* requirement that contract terms always be read and understood in order for them to become legally binding. If an individual representing a company signs a contract without reading or understanding the terms (which often happens even in business-to-business dealings, in particular with click-through agreements and STCs), the company can still become bound by those terms. Clearly there is a need for business, project, risk, contract, and legal professionals—and for all participants in a supply chain—to work together. If this does not happen and a problem arises, the ultimate result will be conflict, as the parties argue that the responsibility lies with someone else.

THE CONTRACT RISK AND OPPORTUNITY MANAGEMENT PLAN

With all these processes and principles, it is easy to feel overwhelmed. How can you implement systematic contract risk management? How can you start using your contracting processes and documents *systematically* and *proactively* to (1) decrease the possibility and impact of failure and negative events, (2) increase the possibility and impact of business success and positive events, and (3) enable sound risk taking, which includes balancing risk with reward? To do so, you need a plan. This is what the *Contract Risk and Opportunity Management Plan* is designed to accomplish.

WHY DO YOU NEED A PLAN?

Many professionals already use contracts for risk management purposes and possess considerable skills at doing so. Most do it intuitively, as part of good business practice, good project management, or good lawyering. But in today's business, individual skills are not always sufficient to manage an organization's contract risks and opportunities. Contract risk identification should be undertaken by the relevant members of the business or project team, not just by the "experts." It should be undertaken in the context of the other issues and risks facing the team, whose members (rather than the "experts") will be in charge of managing the risks during contract implementation. To support seamless risk recognition, review, and response, it is useful to have a plan in place. Every plan does not have to be great or flawless; even an imperfect plan can be better than nothing.

Albert Szent-Gyorti, Nobel Laureate in medicine, tells the story of a military reconnaissance team that was lost in the Swiss Alps following a snowstorm. The soldiers had given up hope of returning to their main unit alive when one of them discovered a map in their equipment. Having the map calmed the soldiers and, with the sense of direction provided by the map, they found their main unit. Upon their return, they showed the map to their lieutenant, who discovered that it was a map of the Pyrenees, rather than the Alps.[11]

This story illustrates that a leader does not need a perfect plan to calm employees and get them moving in the right direction. Simply having a plan is often enough to inspire action that can lead to positive results. As noted by Karl Weick, a faculty

---

11   Weick, K.E. (1995) *Sensemaking in Organizations*. Foundations for Organizational Science. Thousand Oaks, CA: Sage, pp. 54–5.

member at the Ross School of Business at the University of Michigan and one of the world's leading organizational theorists:

> *Followers are often lost and even the leader is not sure where to go. All the leaders know is that the plan or the map they have in front of them is not sufficient to get them out. What the leader has to do, when faced with this situation, is instill some confidence in people, get them moving in some general direction, and be sure they look closely at cues created by their actions so that they learn where they were and get some better idea of where they are and where they want to be.*[12]

APPLYING THE FOUR STEPS OF THE PLAN

The Contract Risk and Opportunity Management Plan is a four-step process that can be applied to systematic risk and opportunity management at any stage of a contract's lifecycle. For complex projects, the plan should be used as early as possible, preferably at the bid or solicitation planning stage when laying the foundation for the deal, because this is where the structure and contents of the contract begin to take shape. The Plan can also be applied at the contract preparation, design, and negotiation stage—for instance, when reviewing proposed solicitation and bid documents or contract proposals and individual clauses in those documents, and when reviewing or auditing a company's standard forms, models, templates and standard terms and conditions. It can also be used to secure a successful handoff to a new team during the different phases of the contract lifecycle. While the Plan can be used by individuals, the best results are achieved

---

12   Weick 1995, p. 55.

when it is used by a team. The four principal steps of the Plan are as follows:

STEP ONE: BECOME CONTRACTUALLY LITERATE

This step starts with an understanding of the business and legal dimensions of contracts and the impact of contracts on successful business outcomes as well as the related risks. It requires a basic understanding of the laws that are relevant to the company's business deals and relationships. This step, which is the foundation for the success of the entire plan, goes beyond having contracts or legal experts available when an issue arises. It involves understanding when contracts are formed, even when a document bearing such title is not present; understanding both their *visible* and *invisible* terms; exercising informed judgment when negotiating and working with them; and knowing when professional legal help is (and is not) required.[13]

STEP TWO: RECOGNIZE CONTRACT RISKS AND OPPORTUNITIES

The second step focuses on recognizing and describing relevant risks and opportunities. This requires identifying sources of risk and opportunity, their *causes*, and potential *consequences*. But first, the *objectives* of the contractual arrangement—business objectives and legal objectives—must be determined.

The objective of completing a delivery project on time provides a simple example. Assume that we work for a supplier of production equipment that has a contract with a customer.

---

13   For visible and invisible terms and the different aspects of contract literacy, see Chapters 2, 4 and 5 of this volume.

The completion date is approaching, and certain tailor-made components that are on the critical path are missing. Based on earlier experience with similar projects, we know that our on-time delivery depends on the timely arrival of those tailor-made components. We also know that our component suppliers do not always understand the time and place of delivery the way we do, despite the fact that we use Incoterms trade terms in our orders. We will use this chain of events— our component supplier's late delivery causing our project completion to be late—as the *cause* of risk to illustrate Steps two to four.

Having identified the cause, we now turn to identifying the potential *consequences* of the risk materializing. We might have access to a contract summary or a review checklist that will help us ask the right questions and find the answers. Risk lists and review checklists are helpful when identifying potential sources and consequences of risk. Figure 6.2 is an extract from a sample contract risk list related to the consequences of breach, namely liabilities and remedies.

In our simplified example, let us assume that we identify two potential consequences of the risk of delay in delivery: the customer will not pay us on time, leading to delay of cash flow, and the customer will claim compensation from us for the loss it suffers due to our delay. While we have chosen to focus on this one risk in our example, Step Two will normally result in a long list of risks and opportunities that need to be prioritized. This is the goal of Step Three.

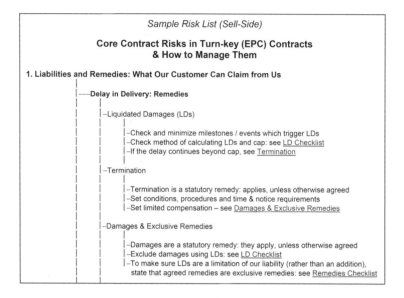

Figure 6.2   Extract from a supplier's contract risk list

STEP THREE: REVIEW CONTRACT RISKS AND OPPORTUNITIES

After identifying the causes and consequences of risks and opportunities in Step Two, the third step seeks to analyze them to understand their nature and to prioritize them by determining their *level* (sometimes called the *magnitude* or *significance*), often expressed in terms of a combination of the *consequences* (or *impact*) of an event and the associated *likelihood* (or *probability*) of its occurrence. The results can be illustrated in a 3 × 3 (or 5 × 5) *cube* or *matrix*, where the impact and probability of an event are assigned high, medium and low ratings or described with numerical values, using 1 for low and 3 (or 5) for high. In connection with risks, the *likelihood* can be described as remote (or rare), unlikely, possible, likely, or very likely. The *consequences* can be described as minimal (or insignificant), minor, moderate, major, or catastrophic, leading to the risks being qualified as low, medium, high, or very high.[14]

The risk or opportunity cube (or matrix) is especially useful for prioritizing risks and opportunities for further action— for example, by accepting those risks and omitting those opportunities that are qualified as low and medium, but addressing the ones that are shown as high or very high. A sample 5 × 5 risk cube and opportunity cube are shown in Figure 6.3. The risk cube illustrates likelihood versus consequence, the opportunity cube likelihood versus benefit.

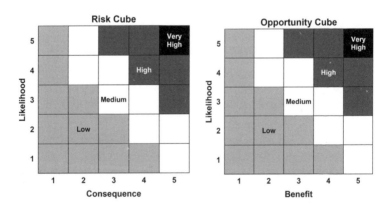

Figure 6.3   A risk cube and an opportunity cube

---

14   See, for example, Mahler 2010, p. 47. In the case study conducted by Mahler, using the standard terms and conditions of a sales contract as the basis, the team's risk identification resulted in a list of initially 88 risks, each of which was listed in a risk register. Having analyzed and scored the risks, the list was reduced to a total of 35 risks, comprising 12 high, 16 medium and 7 low risks. The reduction was achieved by omitting the lowest risks and those which seemed irrelevant for other reasons. See Mahler 2010, p. 235.

Using our example of a delay in delivery, we begin by assessing the magnitude of the *consequences* of the risk. Here, we would examine the two contracts more closely, starting with the one that we have with the customer and then repeating the exercise with the contract with our component supplier to determine what has been agreed between the respective parties (the visible terms). Where there are gaps in the contract, we also need to understand what the applicable law says about the issue at hand (the invisible terms).

When assessing magnitude, a review checklist is useful in focusing attention on *visible* and *invisible* terms. The list might be presented in the form of questions calling for a yes/no answer, as illustrated by Table 6.1.

Table 6.1   Extract from a supplier's quotation/ contract review list

Magnitude of the consequences of delay in delivery	Yes	No
Are the consequences of delay in delivery specified in the quotation/contract itself or in the STCs that are made part thereof?		
Is there an effective cap/maximum for liability for delay in delivery? Is that maximum acceptable, considering the price and profit margin?		
If liquidated damages are agreed, are other remedies effectively excluded?		

Using our example, let us assume that it turns out that our contract with the customer contains a seven-day grace period but does not contain a limitation of liability. The customer is estimated to suffer a considerable loss (loss of production and high claims from its own customers) due to the delay of our delivery, and is known for aggressively exercising its rights even through litigation. In our contract with our component supplier, we realize that there is a low limit to that supplier's liability towards us. Like most businesses, we have no insurance coverage for these kinds of situations; we are on our own. It the risk materializes, there will be no profit on this contract. In addition, if the customer's claim for damages is successful, this can lead to a major loss that has a strategic impact. The *consequence* is thus estimated to be major and rated at 4.[15] Let us assume that the *likelihood* of the risk materializing—that is, our delivery being more than 7 days late—is estimated at 5 (very likely), bringing our estimated risk level (likelihood 5 × consequence 4) to 20, high priority. Table 6.2 shows an extract from a sample Risk Matrix completed from our hypothetical equipment supplier's point of view.

We would then analyze other risks—-along with their causes and consequences—we have identified by using the risk matrix. Our delay example is probably among the highest-ranking risks, one that should receive a high priority. While we should have used the risk matrix earlier when planning the project and reviewing the sales and procurement documents, this process does present a learning opportunity for the future. When using the matrix as a team discussion facilitation tool, we will gain new insights into areas that need improvement.

---

15   In the case study conducted by Mahler, using a sales contract as the basis, the consequence values were described as follows: insignificant: the influence on this sales contract can be neglected; minor: a limited reduction of this sales contract's profitability; moderate: a considerable reduction of the sales contract's profitability; major: no profit in this contract or major loss that has a strategic impact on the division; and catastrophic: this would have a strategic impact on the company or even endanger the company's existence. See Mahler 2010, pp. 286–7.

Table 6.2   Extract from a supplier's risk matrix

Risk	Cause	Impact	Likelihood 1–5	Impact 1–5	Ranking	Priority
Delay of completion by more than 7 days	Component supplier's late delivery of critical component	Delay of cash-flow	5	4	20	High
	Misunderstanding of the time and terms of delivery	Customer claims for compensation				
	Too tight schedule	Additional costs				

STEP FOUR: RESPOND TO CONTRACT RISKS AND OPPORTUNITIES

The fourth and final step in the plan is *risk response* (also known as *risk treatment*). At this step we develop options and actions to address the highest-ranking risks and opportunities and put in place controls to remove or reduce threats (or, in case of opportunities, to strengthen their drivers and enhance the opportunities). Developing, selecting and implementing risk controls can be as simple as one person monitoring a to-do list. But sometimes it involves a team of experts, a full list of all identified risks and a record of the responses. The optimum is perhaps somewhere in the middle: a record of what is needed to manage the risks through monitoring and control, without too much paperwork. Again, both *likelihood* and *consequences* matter. The options generally available for risk response include the following:

- accept or retain the risk

- reduce the likelihood of the risk occurring

- reduce the consequences of the risk occurring

- transfer or share the risk

- avoid the risk.[16]

---

16   In connection with opportunities, the response options could include the following: accept or retain the opportunity, increase its likelihood or consequences, exploit, share, or enhance the opportunity. A key concept of opportunity engineering is making uncertainty work for you rather than against you. See, generally, van Putten, A.B. and MacMillan, I.C. (2009) *Unlocking Opportunities for Growth. How to Profit from Uncertainty While Limiting Your Risk.* Upper Saddle River, NJ: Wharton School Publishing.

Before committing to a contract, all options related to contract risk response are open. After a contract is made, there are fewer options. Transferring the risk might mean transferring it to another party, such as a customer, supplier, subcontractor, or insurance company. The risk might also be shared and managed together, which in many cases of mutual dependence is the ideal option. As already noted, risk transfer does not mean that the risk goes away; in reality it still usually results in shared risk. Avoiding the risk might mean deciding not to proceed—for example, deciding not to bid or order, or to walk away from a proposed deal. It may also mean changing the roles and responsibilities in a contract.

When discussing contract risks, contractual responses may come to mind first. In addition to frequently-used liabilities and indemnities clauses, these responses might include contract provisions such as grace periods, force majeure, and timing of notices and claims. Yet other kinds of responses, such as relational controls or performance controls, might be more effective than contractual responses. In our example, while it is not realistic to attempt to change the contractual provisions at this point, reducing the likelihood and the impact through other means remains an option.

The likelihood of a risk occurring can be reduced in various ways, depending on the risk. Table 6.3 shows an extract from a sample Risk Response Plan (sometimes also called Risk Register) completed from our hypothetical equipment supplier's point of view. The Risk Response Plan builds on (and may be part of) the Risk Matrix (see Table 6.2) or a separate document. In addition to the main headings and information found in Table 6.2 it includes the response plan, the name or job function of the risk owner and responsible person(s), and the schedule for the response as well as room for follow-up to make sure the plan has been implemented.

Table 6.3 Extract from a supplier's risk response plan

Risk	Cause	Impact	Priority	Response plan	Risk owner / responsible persons	By Date	Done Yes/No
Delay of completion by more than 7 days	Component supplier's late delivery of critical component Misunderstanding of the time and terms of delivery ...	Delay of cash-flow Customer claims for compensation ...	High	1. Notify customer of possible delay; request extension or seek to change contract if possible.	Name		
				2. Monitor component supplier's timely preparation and performance.	Name		
				3. Seek to obtain missing components from another source.	Name		
				4. Follow up all subs' actual understanding of their contracts' time and terms of delivery.	Name		

Ideally, generating ideas for risk responses and controls is a team effort. Visual tools such as the bow-tie diagram[17] can be used to help team members see the big picture and identify what needs to be done to deal effectively with the risk before and after the event. The plan may also include contingency or fallback plans for each risk, along with the trigger for those plans. Probably the most important piece of information in this plan is the name of the person accountable for the risk, the "risk owner" and the names of those in charge of implementing the response plan. These persons need to accept accountability and may need resources and support.

The next action within Step Four is to implement the plan and then to monitor and review its success. Depending on the nature of the business and projects, the monitoring can be continuous, and reviews of the recognized risks and selected responses can be carried out at regular intervals. The tools and information collected may also be used at the end of each project to ensure that the organization learns from its successes and failures.

This example, if it were real, would teach the equipment supplier important lessons that should be documented and shared when preparing future quotations and contracts. The lessons include developing a contracting policy; using risk lists and other risk review and management tools at the earliest possible stage, *before* committing to a contract; reviewing and synchronizing contracts in the supply chain; securing a seamless flow-through of commitments from customers on one side to component suppliers and other subcontractors on the other; and noting potential gaps in contracts and *back-to-back* provisions that transfer (or should transfer) to

---

17   Visual tools are discussed later in this chapter. For the bow-tie diagram, see Figure 6.6.

subcontractors the obligations the company has undertaken in the main contract.

The example also illustrates that contract provisions alone do not remove the cause of the problem or minimize its likelihood. The supplier needs to secure a realistic schedule and clarity as to the parties' (including subcontractors') responsibilities. It needs to implement sound contract and project management practices, integrate sales contracting with procurement, and closely monitor its own and its subcontractors' progress. With regard to the consequences of a delay, the supplier learned a lesson about the importance of clear, understandable contractual provisions dealing with delivery[18] and other obligations, as well as the importance of limitations of liabilities and remedies and procedures for handling problem situations.

CONTRACT MANAGEMENT: OWNERSHIP, ACCOUNTABILITY, AND BEYOND

To manage your contract risks on a continuous basis, you will benefit greatly from a framework that supports the management of your contracts end-to-end. In some countries and cultures, contract management is a well-developed discipline and profession. In others, it is not. In some businesses, the contracting process is well-documented, including identification of the participants in the process and the steps to be taken. In others, it is not.

---

18   For common misunderstandings about what "delivery" means, especially in international trade, and what to do about them, see Haapio, H. (2004) Invisible terms in international contracts and what to do about them. *Contract Management*, July, 32–5, available at http://www.ncmahq.org/files/Articles/81EEB_cm_July04_32.pdf.

As stated in Chapter 3, many business people still see contracting as a series of unconnected steps rather than a process. They lack a holistic view and proper contract management, leading to risky gaps in the contracting process.

Where does your business stand with respect to contract management? You may want to do a quick pulse check. A key control in any process is *clear ownership* of that process. If you examine your organization charts, manuals, job descriptions, approval matrices, and guidelines for authority, can you locate the person to whom the contracting process is assigned? Do you find a single owner or several owners designated by functional responsibility? Are their accountabilities well-defined?

Do you find any owner(s) at all? If not, you are not alone. Many companies are lacking in this respect, or in some of the other aspects of the Top Ten Best Practices in Commercial Contracting identified by the International Association for Contract and Commercial Management (IACCM).

The first item on the list of best practices (Table 6.4) is, unsurprisingly, ownership and accountability for the contracting process. For successful contracting and risk management, *somebody* must take ownership and ensure alignment and adherence, along with overseeing successful handover from one team to another and managing change. *Somebody* must be in charge to ensure that the interests of the different units, functions and professionals are aligned. *Somebody* should establish contracting strategy and make sure that the people involved know why, when, how, and by whom proposals, purchase orders, and contracts are to be initiated, reviewed, and monitored. The responsibilities and accountabilities must be clear.

Table 6.4   IACCM top ten best practices in commercial contracting[19]

1.	Ownership and accountability for the contracting process
2.	Terms and structure audit and update
3.	Integration with Product Lifecycle Management (PLM)
4.	Portfolio risk management
5.	Supply/value chain focus
6.	Electronic contracting strategy
7.	Self-help skills assessment and development tools
8.	Strategically aligned measurements and reporting
9.	Proactive change management
10.	Differentiation and sources of value: awareness and marketing

Contract management has been defined as "the planning, monitoring and control of all aspects of the contract and the motivation of all those involved ... to achieve the contract objectives on time and to the specified cost, quality and performance."[20] According to Tim Cummins, the CEO of the IACCM, the role of contract management is threefold: to secure economic value, to provide a framework for the allocation and management of risk, and to oversee the performance of commitments that reflect a positive brand image.[21] As is

19   Cummins, T. (2006) Best practices in commercial contracting. key initiatives that are driving competitive advantage. In P. Wahlgren and C. Magnusson Sjöberg (Eds.), *A Proactive Approach. Scandinavian Studies in Law*, Volume 49. Stockholm: Stockholm Institute for Scandinavian Law, pp. 131–47, 143–5, available at http://www.scandinavianlaw.se/pdf/49-8.pdf. See also the related *IACCM Top Ten Best Practices in Commercial Contracting – 2006 Status Report*, available (for IACCM members) at http://www.iaccm.com/library/?id=1135.

20   IACCM (2011) *Contract and Commercial Management. The Operational Guide.* Zaltbommel: Van Haren Publishing, p. 617.

21   Cummins, T. (2012) The role of contract management. Commitment Matters Blog, January 19, available at http://contract-matters.com/2012/01/19/the-role-of-contract-management.

obvious from these statements, contract management, project management, and risk management are intertwined, and the success of one is very much dependent on the success of the others.

From a contract risk management perspective, the pre-contract phase is often the most important of all phases of the process. The better the tools, controls, and practices available at the front end of the process, before contract commitments are made, the easier it is to build contract risk management into the process. Ideally all risks inherent in a deal or relationship will be examined *prior to* making a contract—or better still, before making an order or submitting a proposal (or, in procurement, before issuing a request for proposals or order). A supplier should make its bid/no bid decision based on an evaluation of risks in relation to the rewards and opportunities the deal presents. A buyer should make its supplier selection based on, first, which supplier is most likely to succeed and, second, the price and other terms. Both the supplier and the buyer share an interest in developing the terms of their relationship in a manner most likely to bring mutual success and benefits to both.

The fifth item on the list of IACCM Top Ten Best Practices in Commercial Contracting also highlights the importance of contract management and accountability—supply-chain (or value-chain) focus. Many businesses are still struggling to reach a more integrated management across the organization, including sell-side and buy-side commitments and contracts. Effective contract (and contract risk) management requires an alignment of requirements, responsibilities and risks throughout the chain. As already noted, sometimes the most knowledgeable party is better off educating and supporting the others—making it easy for them to succeed—rather than forcing them to make contractual promises they are unable to keep.

Just as the best practices adopted by other areas in a company usually incorporate the latest technology, technology also has the potential to transform the way contracts are created and managed. Today everyone has access to comprehensive commercial off-the-shelf automated forms, templates, clause libraries, and Web-based self-service solutions for request-for-proposal and proposal preparation and contract creation. Businesses can move from manual drafting to automated contract assembly, and develop and use their own computer-based drafting systems.[22]

Comprehensive contract lifecycle management solutions exist that are designed to simplify the management of the contracting process. A Google search using terms such as "automated document assembly," "contract lifecycle management," "contract management solutions," and "enterprise contract management" produces hundreds of thousands of results. White papers and webcasts abound on implementing and selecting such solutions. And there are technology tools in the market that can convert project and contract documents to an easier-to-read format.[23] As technology tools develop and are implemented, businesses will obtain better visibility into

22   For computer-based drafting, see, for example, Quinn, B.C. and Adams, K.A. (2007) Transitioning your contract process from the artistic to the industrial. *ACC Docket*, December, 61–72, available at http://adamsdrafting.com/downloads/Quinn.Adams.ACCDocket.Dec07.pdf.
23   See, for example, McNair, D. (2005a) Contractual risk identification, assessment and management system for the owner. *Contract Management in Practice*, 2(9), November/December, 136–40, available (for IACCM members) at http://www.iaccm.com/library/?id=890, and McNair, D. (2005b) Contractual risk identification, assessment and management system for the contractor. *Contract Management in Practice*, 2(10), December 2005/January 2006, 156–61, available at http://www.iaccm.com/members/library/files/CMP_2_10.pdf.

their contract portfolio, including the risks and opportunities that these contain, making it easier to manage them.

MANAGING RISKS JOINTLY: FROM RISK ALLOCATION TO TRUE RISK MANAGEMENT

Within the risk management field, contracts have been long known to be effective *risk allocation* tools. Discussion of contract risk management in this field has focused on risk transfer, indemnity and hold harmless clauses, along with insurance to cover contractually or otherwise assumed risks. While knowing when and how to use, require and respond to such clauses—or additional insured endorsements, waivers of subrogation, contractual liability coverage, and so on—is important, these issues are quite complex and can easily blur the big picture so that one no longer sees the forest for the trees.

Within the legal field, practitioners typically discuss contract risk in the context of legal risk. Lawyers are often asked to examine the legal aspects of contracts, with limited or no access to information about the operational details of the deal, relationship, or project in question. Their assessment of risks embodies a legal perspective that focuses on *risk allocation, risk transfer*, and *excluding or limiting liability* in the contract, before the contract is executed. They are seldom involved in ensuring delivery of the obligations or monitoring performance, unless a legal dispute arises. The traditional lawyer's focus is on "spotting legal issues" and on contractual mechanisms that can protect the lawyer's client, rather than on the success of the project or the relationship.

In today's extended supply networks, where businesses are increasingly dependent on one another, it is no longer meaningful (if it ever was) to attempt to transfer all risk to the other party. Instead, the focus should be on ways to *manage risk together*. In addition to the parties' focus on *their own* risks and interests, they should ideally engage in *joint* risk management, focusing on the risks to the overall project or venture.

The parties should use their pre-contract processes, negotiations, and contracts to recognize risks together and build in controls that help prevent or minimize the causes, likelihood, and impact of risk. To succeed, parties must even recognize risks that are hidden in boilerplate or invisible terms. Risks must be identified, understood, and acknowledged by both parties, and both need to take part in finding solutions that help mitigate the risks. In addition to pre-contract risk recognition, review and response, the parties should work together during implementation so that risks continue to be mitigated, monitored, and managed throughout the contract lifecycle. A cooperative and relational approach is called for, rather than confrontation and a focus on contractual risk allocation.

The time has come to change the decades-old way of thinking about contractual risk management as contractual risk allocation or contractual risk transfer, which are only a small part of what *true contract risk management* is about. Contracts offer much more for risk management than limitations of liabilities and remedies, indemnity and hold harmless clauses, and so on. A proactive approach necessitates—and enables—a big picture view and can pave the way towards the parties managing risks jointly.

EARLY WARNING SYSTEM AND JOINT RISK MANAGEMENT BUILT INTO THE CONTRACT

Some contracts direct the parties to warn each other of possible problems before they occur, so that they can be avoided or their effects mitigated. The NEC3 family of contracts[24] offers an example by providing for a scheme for the early identification of risks, risk reduction meetings, and a joint risk register.

For example, the NEC3 Supply Contract contains a system under which the supplier is to give an *early warning* of relevant matters that could increase the price, delay delivery, impair the performance of the goods in use, or impair the usefulness of the services to the purchaser. The supplier may give an early warning of any other matter that could increase its total cost. Early warning matters are entered in the *Risk Register*:

> *a register of the risks which are listed in the Contract Data and the risks which the Supply Manager or the Supplier has notified as an early warning matter. It includes a description of the risk and a description of the actions to be taken to avoid or reduce the risk.*[25]

The NEC3 Supply Contract further provides for a *risk reduction meeting* if requested by either party. The purpose of the meeting is for those in attendance to cooperate, make and consider proposals for how the effect of the registered risks can be avoided or reduced, seek solutions that will bring advantage

---

24   The NEC family of contracts consists of several contracts designed for procuring a diverse range of works, services and goods. Originally launched in 1993, and then known as the "New Engineering Contract," the NEC has been praised for its collaborative and integrated working approach to procurement. See NEC Products, available at http://www.neccontract.com/products/index.asp.

25   See NEC3 Supply Contract Clause 11, Identified and defined terms.

to all those who will be affected, and decide on the actions that will be taken and who will take them.[26]

This approach provides an opportunity for the parties to discuss and resolve matters in an efficient manner as they seek to prevent or minimize problems. It is a clear departure from the usual approach where the supplier (or contractor) serves formal notices and the parties prepare for claims and disputes. The implementation of NEC3 contracts has resulted in major benefits for projects both nationally and internationally in terms of time, cost savings and improved quality.[27]

THE CHALLENGE: ENGAGING PEOPLE AND COMMUNICATING CONTRACTS

As noted in earlier chapters, contracts themselves—including their individual terms or wording—are seldom the real sources of contract risk. The biggest contract risks are related to people's perceptions, expectations, and feelings of disappointment or injury. Often people do not simply expect their contractual provisions to be enforced; they expect their beliefs and understandings of these provisions to be enforced. These understandings are sometimes different from what the text of the contract and its legal interpretation provide.

One reason for this is that people might not read contracts. Even if they do, they might not understand them. They may rely on verbal promises the contract text does not include or on what they believe to be industry practice. The

---

26   See NEC3 Supply Contract Clause 16, Early warning.
27   What is the NEC? Promoting best practice procurement. Achieving excellence in the procurement of Works, Services and Supply. NEC, available at http://www.neccontract.com/documents/WhatistheNEC.pdf.

legal interpretation and literal enforcement of contractual requirements, rights, responsibilities, and remedies may differ from people's beliefs and predictions.

Contract risk management should focus on aligning the contract with the parties' expectations of the deal or relationship. The contract should reflect the *real deal*. In addition, to make sure the contract is implemented successfully, the contract should be clear and understandable. Business success often depends on how well the people implementing the contract understand the contractual requirements, roles, and responsibilities. If these are fulfilled as the parties intended, there is little (if any) need to rely on the clauses dealing with liabilities or remedies (or their limitations).

Sometimes contracts cover complex projects and topics no single professional can master. Sometimes they use terminology that is incomprehensible to the non-expert. Often they are voluminous, dense documents that touch many professions and disciplines. Contract risk and opportunity management can only succeed when the different stakeholders collaborate, which inevitably leads to challenges related to communication.

A WAY TO MEET THE CHALLENGE: VISUALIZATION

If business and project managers see contracts as a necessary evil and sources of excessive bureaucracy, they will look for ways around contracts. If they see contracts merely as legal tools and as tools for self-defense in conflict situations, they will overlook opportunities to use contracts as risk management tools or enablers of successful project implementation. Many current perceptions are not helpful for using contracts successfully. Contract visualization is a tool that can overcome these perceptions by simplifying and demystifying contracts.

THE CONTRACT ELEPHANT: DIFFERENT VIEWERS HAVE DIFFERENT LENSES AND BLIND SPOTS

Diagrams and visual tools are frequently used in project and risk management, quality control, systems engineering, reliability engineering, and operations management to convey complex messages and help people understand them. Why not extend the method to contracts and contracting? Why not use *visualization*—images, charts, diagrams, timelines, and so on—to communicate contract-related messages? Why not be even a bit more playful when communicating them? The Contract Elephant depicted below (Figure 6.4) and the Hand Tool a little later in this chapter (Figure 6.5) offer a good starting point.

Figure 6.4 illustrates the different lenses through which different professionals may view contracts. It is based on the tale of the blind men and an elephant that is often used to illustrate a range of different "truths" and the relativism of truth. While there are many versions of the tale, the basic storyline is about a group of blind men who touch an elephant to learn what it is like. Each of them feels a different part, but only one part. When telling the others what an elephant is like they soon learn that they do not agree. The stories differ in how the conflict is resolved. What the story tells us is that it is important to learn that our own experience may not represent the whole truth and that we must show respect for different perspectives and communicate and collaborate to understand the full picture, in this case, the full (contract) elephant.

The Contract Elephant

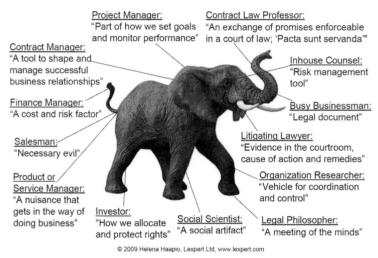

Project Manager:
"Part of how we set goals and monitor performance"

Contract Law Professor:
"An exchange of promises enforceable in a court of law; 'Pacta sunt servanda'"

Contract Manager:
"A tool to shape and manage successful business relationships"

Inhouse Counsel:
"Risk management tool"

Finance Manager:
"A cost and risk factor"

Busy Businessman:
"Legal document"

Salesman:
"Necessary evil"

Litigating Lawyer:
"Evidence in the courtroom, cause of action and remedies"

Product or Service Manager:
"A nuisance that gets in the way of doing business"

Organization Researcher:
"Vehicle for coordination and control"

Investor:
"How we allocate and protect rights"

Social Scientist:
"A social artifact"

Legal Philosopher:
"A meeting of the minds"

© 2009 Helena Haapio, Lexpert Ltd, www.lexpert.com

Figure 6.4   The contract elephant

Ideally, each professional working with contracts recognizes or at least is familiar with the other perspectives or lenses. Yet that is seldom the case. The typical "lawyer's lens" may focus on worst case scenarios, liability exposure, and how the contract will be used as evidence (and provide winning arguments) in court. This focus will then lead to the lawyer drafting documents that in the eyes of business folks are a necessary evil, a nuisance that gets in the way of doing business.

A visual approach to contracts has the potential to change the picture. Visualization offers a way to build a bridge between business and legal needs and to enhance communication among managers, engineers, and their legal advisors. It can enhance managerial–legal decision making and help combine various perspectives. Using images can make it easier to communicate and "sell" contracts, internally and externally— and easier for everyone involved to understand and to translate contracts into desired action and outcomes.[28] Flowcharts, timelines, and mind maps can help evaluate a proposed transaction or relationship (or network of transactions and relationships), assess its risks and opportunities, and co-create tools to control them in new ways.

Project management was one of the early adapters of visualization. The book *Visualizing Project Management*[29] (already in its third edition) illustrates that complex systems do not require complex project management and that visualization is a powerful technique for achieving high performance.

Knowledge visualization in the context of risk management is not new either. At the University of St.Gallen Institute for Media and Communications Management, research findings related to risk communication and communication of knowledge between experts and decision makers illustrate the benefits—and also the risks—related to visualization in contexts where interaction and cross-communication

---

28   See, for example, Finnegan, M. and Haapio, H. (2012) Communicating contracts in split seconds: using visual tools to make leadership pay attention. *Contract Management*, July, 26–43, available at http://www.ncmahq.org/files/Articles/CM0712%20 -%2026-43.pdf, and Passera, S. and Haapio H. (2011) User-centered contract design: new directions in the quest for simpler contracting. In R.F. Henschel (Ed.), *Proceedings of the 2011 IACCM Academic Symposium for Contract and Commercial Management, Tempe (AZ), USA, 26 October 2011*. Ridgefield, CT: The International Association for Contract and Commercial Management, pp. 80–97, available at http://www.iaccm.com/admin/docs/ docs/HH_Paper.pdf.
29   Forsberg, K., Mooz, H. and Cotterman, H. (2005) *Visualizing Project Management*, 3rd edn. Hoboken, NJ: John Wiley & Sons Ltd.

are required when each stakeholder only has a fragmented understanding of the issues involved.[30]

Other business professionals use visuals to present their thoughts and ideas. Business development managers use proposal graphics to illustrate and sell ideas.[31] Product and service development professionals and project managers use process flow diagrams and swim lanes to visualize business processes that involve more than one department (for example, customer, sales, contracts, legal, and fulfillment) to clarify the sequence of events and how information or material passes between sub-processes. Swim lanes can be used to illustrate the steps and who is responsible for each one, as well as how delays and mistakes are most likely to occur.[32]

Visualization was also incorporated into research related to legal risks conducted at the University of Oslo Faculty of Law. In a case study, a group of lawyers, managers, and engineers were asked to analyze the risks related to a contract proposal using a method based on graphical language and diagrams.[33] The case study showed that graphical language is helpful in

---

30   See Eppler, M.J. (2004) *Knowledge Communication Problems between Experts and Managers. An Analysis of Knowledge Transfer in Decision Processes.* Paper # 1/2004, May 2004, available at http://doc.rero.ch/lm.php?url=1000,42,6,20051020101029-UL/1_ wpca0401.pdf, and Eppler, M.J. and Aeschimann, M. (2008) *Envisioning Risk. A Systematic Framework for Risk Visualization in Risk Management and Communication.* ICA Working Paper 5/2008, and other resources available at USI HSG Knowledge Communication— Publications at http://www.knowledge-communication.org/publications.html.
31   See, for example, Newman, L. (2011) *Shipley Proposal Guide*, 4th edn. Kaysville, UT: Shipley Associates, pp. 70–79.
32   For an example, see the Wikipedia entry Swim lane, available at http://en.wikipedia.org/wiki/Swim_lane.
33   Mahler 2010, pp. 237–62. The case study was carried out for a corporation that supplies production goods to a manufacturer. The risk assessment team consisted of several lawyers, a financial expert, and two technical experts, as well as three business managers. The team analyzed the risks related to the STCs of one of the corporation's customers in the context of a major long-term production contract. The assessment was carried out in order to draft a contracting policy for future contract negotiations.

communicating risk among the participants. The non-lawyers in particular were enthusiastic about the use of the graphical models. Without these models, many of them found the contract documents difficult to understand and difficult to relate to their business perspective. The graphical models helped them to assess the impact of the contract clauses.[34] However, the need for simplicity and usability revealed some limitations and the need for a combination of graphical and natural language for improved decision making. The research also confirms that one challenge for contractual risk management is to integrate the traditional legal risk handling perspective with the risk management approaches in other disciplines.[35]

THE HAND TOOL: A SIMPLE TOOL FOR BETTER CONTRACT REVIEW AND RISK CONTROL

While contracts always have a legal dimension, it has been noted that on average, nearly 80 percent of the terms in business-to-business contracts are *not* really areas of significant legal concern. Instead, most terms are business and financial, including statements of work, specifications and service-level agreements.[36]

The contract needs to provide clarity as to the roles and responsibilities of the parties, scope of the delivery, implementation, and pricing. The contract should specify details regarding *what, where, when* and *how*. It also needs

---

34   Mahler 2010, p. 252.
35   Mahler 2010, pp. 75 and 261–2. See also Mahler, T. (2008) The state of the art of contractual risk management methodologies. In H. Haapio (Ed.), *A Proactive Approach to Contracting and Law*. Turku: Turku University of Applied Sciences, pp. 57–74.
36   Cummins, T. (2003) *Contracting as a Strategic Competence*. International Association for Contract and Commercial Management IACCM, available at http://www.iaccm.com/library/nonphp/contracting.pdf.

to clarify what happens if either party cannot or does not perform.

Experience and research show that the same issues repeat themselves and create problems in similar contracting situations. Focusing business, technical and legal resources on such issues and developing contractual and business solutions to resolve them is well worth the effort. For instance, if technical specifications, work scope definition, or task allocation are unclear, problems will follow. In the words of Mark Grossman,

> taking time at the beginning to work out detailed design specs is equally important to both sides of the development deal. It's the only way to be sure everyone's on the same page, that there's been a meeting of the minds as to what the software should do and how. And that's also the only way both sides will ever be able to walk away from a development project looking forward to doing another one together.[37]

Even a simple from of visualization, a "hand tool" (Figure 6.5), can prevent unnecessary problems. It lists the trivial-sounding but crucial questions that must be answered when creating or reviewing obligations: who/which party shall do—what—where—when—how—and, last but not least, what if/what if not. This simple hand tool has proven to work in practice, both on the sell-side and on the buy-side. If the parties remember to go through the questions and address them when creating, amending, or passing on contractual obligations, a number of

---

37   For instance, in software development contracts, design specifications, flexible pricing, and performance standards tend to become frequent points of contention. See Grossman, M. (2012) *Software Development Contracts*. Tannenbaum Helpern Syracuse & Hirschtritt LLP, available at http://www.thsh.com/Publications/Articles-by-Topic/Technology-Telecom-and-Outsourcing/Software-Development-Contracts.aspx.

potential pitfalls can be avoided and contract reviews and risk control measures can be improved. Much more sophisticated tools and checklists exist—yet few are as easy to remember and carry around.

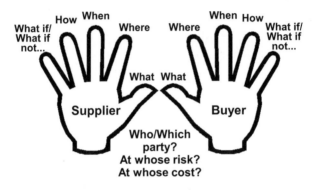

Figure 6.5   The hand tool

THE BOW-TIE DIAGRAM: A WAY TO VISUALIZE RISKS AND WAYS TO CONTROL THEM

A more sophisticated form of visualization, the bow-tie diagram, is shown in Figure 6.6. As shown in the figure, the diagram is shaped like a bow-tie, showing a clear differentiation between proactive and reactive actions. In its simplest form the bow-tie diagram shows causes (risk sources) on the left-hand side, the undesirable event in the middle, and the consequences that may follow from the event on the right. The diagram can be used to help identify what needs to be done to deal effectively with the risk before and after the event. Actions on both sides—proactive controls and reactive controls—can ideally be built in at the contract planning and design stage.

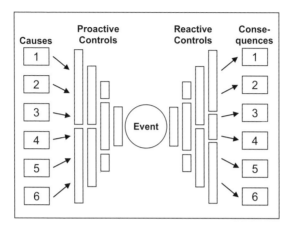

Figure 6.6   The bow-tie diagram

A bow-tie diagram can be used to capture and share different views and aspects of risks, their causes and consequences, and to facilitate discussion of risk assessment. As there is often a whole spectrum of possible causes and potential outcomes, the bow tie is useful in focusing on the big picture.

A similar image and the metaphor of Swiss cheese is used in the context of aviation safety, engineering, and health care. The basic idea is that most serious accidents do not result from a single failure or error; they usually come from an error whose consequences were permitted to be amplified either by additional faults or errors, or by the absence (or failure) of a secondary wall of defense.[38] The different defenses can be modeled as a series of barriers, represented as slices of Swiss

38   See, for example, Dauer, E.A. (2006) The role of culture in legal risk management. In P. Wahlgren and C. Magnusson Sjöberg (Eds.), *A Proactive Approach. Scandinavian Studies in Law*, Volume 49. Stockholm: Stockholm Institute for Scandinavian Law, pp. 93–108, 107–8, available at http://www.scandinavianlaw.se/pdf/49-6.pdf.

cheese. The holes in the cheese slices vary in size and position. The system as a whole fails when all of the holes in each of the slices align, permitting the hazard to pass through all of the holes in all of the defenses. If any one of them had stopped the flow, the failure would not have occurred.[39]

Both the bow tie and the Swiss cheese images can be applied to various causes of contract risks. They can be applied to minimize and control not only the causes but also the likelihood and the consequences of undesirable events. When inserted into a bow tie, both the proactive and reactive controls that contracts can provide become visible. In this way, parties realize that contracts are more than risk allocation tools or reactive sources of defense; they are true risk management tools that the parties can use to manage risk together.

THE TIMELINES THAT COULD HAVE PREVENTED A MULTI-MILLION DOLLAR DISPUTE

At times, the interests of the parties to a contract negotiation are widely misaligned. One party wishes to have a long-term commitment, while the other wishes to be able to walk away from the deal on short notice. The parties' different expectations relating to the intended duration of their relationship can lead to a less than amicable end of the contract. Due to their different perceptions, the parties are likely to differ on the interpretation of contract terms, especially those that are poorly written.

---

39   For examples, see Figures 3 and 6 in Reason, J., Hollnagel, E. and Paries, J. (2006) *Revisiting the "Swiss Cheese" Model of Accidents*. EEC Note No. 13/06. European Organisation for the Safety of Air Navigation, EUROCONTROL, 6 and 10, available at http://publish.eurocontrol.int/eec/gallery/content/public/document/eec/report/2006/017_Swiss_Cheese_Model.pdf.

In the following case study from Canada, a termination clause was interpreted differently by the two parties. Ideally the parties would have discovered their different views of the contract at the negotiation stage. But they did not. In this case, lack of clarity lead to an 18-month dispute over the meaning of a single comma in a clause. More than $2 million Canadian was at stake. In this case, a simple visualization could have helped to prevent a major legal battle.

In 2002, Rogers Cable Communications Inc. (Rogers) entered into a Support Structure Agreement (SSA) with Aliant Telecom Inc. (Aliant), in which Aliant gave Rogers access to and use of certain telephone poles at a fixed rate. In order to raise its rates in 2005 from $9.60 per pole to $28.05 per pole (which would have increased Rogers' costs by about $2.13 million Canadian),[40] Aliant gave Rogers one year's notice to terminate the contract. Rogers objected, stating that the contract had a minimum duration of five years. The misunderstanding revolved around a single clause in the SSA:

> *8.1 This agreement shall be effective from the date it is made and shall continue in force for a period of five (5) years from the date it is made, and thereafter for successive five (5) year terms, unless and until terminated by one year prior notice in writing by either party.*

As regards the initial term of the agreement, Rogers thought that it had a five-year deal. Aliant was of the view that even within this initial term, the SSA could be terminated at any

---

40   See Robertson, G. (2006) Comma quirk irks Rogers. *The Globe and Mail*, 6 August 2006, available at http://m.theglobeandmail.com/report-on-business/comma-quirk-irks-rogers/article1101686/?service=mobile and Austen, I. (2006) The comma that costs 1 million dollars (Canadian). *New York Times*, 25 October, available at http://www.nytimes.com/2006/10/25/business/worldbusiness/25comma.html?_r=1.

time with one year's notice. The validity of the agreement and the money at stake all came down the meaning of the final comma. In 2006, the Canadian authority CRTC (Canadian Radio-Television and Telecommunications Commission) sided with Aliant: "Based on the rules of punctuation," it stated, "the plain and ordinary meaning of section 8.1 of the SSA allows for the termination of the SSA at any time, without cause, upon one year's written notice."[41]

However, the dispute did not end there. The parties' agreement was based on a model SSA that had been issued by the CRTC in both English and French. There was a difference between the French and English language versions of section 8.1. In response to Rogers' appeal, the CRTC reviewed the French-language version of the model SSA and sided with Rogers, deciding that the contract ran for a five-year initial term and could not be terminated unilaterally before the expiration of the first term.[42]

One would think that the duration of a contract is of such great importance that the parties and their lawyers would make sure that the parties' intent is clearly stated in the contract. In this case, neither party had drafted the problematic clause; they had relied on a model SSA. In hindsight, it is easy to say that they should have closely examined the clause before setting the price and other terms and signing the agreement. Also, the drafters of the SSA model form should have used clearer language. Breaking the clause into two sentences would have been a way to avoid the ambiguity.[43] Had the language been

---

41   Telecom Decision CRTC 2006-45, Ottawa, 28 July 2006, Sections 27–30, available at http://www.crtc.gc.ca/eng/archive/2006/dt2006-45.htm.
42   Telecom Decision CRTC 2007-75, Ottawa, 20 August 2007, available at http://www.crtc.gc.ca/eng/archive/2007/dt2007-75.htm.
43   For drafting suggestions, see Adams, K. (2006) Costly drafting errors, part 1—Rogers Communications and Aliant. AdamsDrafting Blog, 7 August, available at http://

clearer, the parties would probably have noticed upfront their differing understandings. Expectations are hard to manage or align if they are not visible.

Simple timelines, as in the chart in Figure 6.7, would have shown the parties their different understandings. This would have allowed them, during the negotiations, to come to a mutual understanding and remove the ambiguity. A simple chart could have prevented the dispute and saved the parties considerable time and legal fees in resolving the dispute.

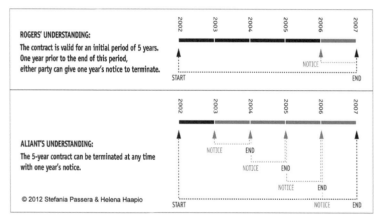

Figure 6.7 **Two timelines that make different understandings visible**[44]

www.adamsdrafting.com/2006/08/07/costly-drafting-errors-part-1 and other postings by Ken Adams at http://www.adamsdrafting.com and at http://www.koncision.com/category/blog/.

44   Haapio, H. (2011) Contract clarity through visualization—preliminary observations and experiments. In E. Banissi et al. (Eds.), *Proceedings of the 15th International Conference on Information Visualisation, IV2011 (London 13–15 July 2011)*. Los Alamitos, CA: IEEE Computer Society, pp. 337–42, 339. See also Passera, S. and Haapio, H. (2011) Facilitating collaboration through contract visualization and modularization. In A. Dittmar and P. Forbrig (Eds.), *Designing Collaborative Activities. ECCE 2011 European Conference on Cognitive Ergonomics 2011—The 29th annual conference of the European Association on Cognitive Ergonomics, August 24–26, 2011, Rostock, Germany*. Rostock:

Case law provides many similar examples illustrating that successful contracts cannot be based on one-sided assumptions, unexpressed expectations, or unclear goals. Many of these problems could have been prevented had the parties taken the time to review, align, and articulate their expectations. If their interests cannot be aligned, they should walk away and find another contract partner. In the words of Louis M. Brown, the Father of Preventive Law: "It usually costs less to avoid getting into trouble than to pay for getting out of trouble."[45]

As in all communication, clarity of thought is required first. To achieve desired results, the results should be clear. If they are not clear, how can they be shared, articulated in a contract, and achieved? Lack of clarity can be a major source of risk. The path to *results* begins from clarity of thought and expression and then, ideally, flows as follows:[46]

Clarity → Understanding → Fast decisions → Action → Results

Research shows that visual elements can play an important role in enhancing clarity, supporting understanding, sharing knowledge, and retaining information. Visualizations have an impact on attitude and behaviour, and they can be used in business to leverage a party's emotional response and cognitive abilities to understand the content.[47]

Universität Rostock, pp. 57–60; and Austen 2006. Visualization reprinted with the permission of Stefania Passera.
45   Brown, L.M. (1950) *Preventive Law*. New York, NY: Prentice-Hall, Inc., p. 3.
46   Eppler, M. (2011) Why care about clarity? Because it leads to results. Presentation How to be CLEAR in Complex Corporate Communication at Aalto University Business School on 24 January 2011, citing Xplane, Inc.
47   Eppler, M.J. and Bischof, N. (2011) *From Complex to Clear. Managing Clarity in Corporate Communication*. Institute for Media and Communication Management,

One way to quickly understand a particular contract or contract clause is to use one of the tools available on the Internet, such as Wordle,[48] to create a "word cloud," a visualization based on the frequency of words. Words that appear more frequently in the text are rendered in a larger font. In contracts, it is not the frequency of the words that matters, of course; it is what the terms actually say. Yet it is often informative to see the words that stand out—often words like damages, liquidated damages, compensation, notice, and so on.

A NEW MINDSET ENABLES BETTER DECISIONS AND RESULTS

It has been said that the legal profession has excelled in applying a "belt and suspenders" approach to contracts, especially to risk transfer and liability clauses drafted (presumably) for one party's benefit. On the other hand, empirical research and experience tell us that these clauses are not always used in practice—at least as long as businesses resolve issues among themselves and not through legal means. In Stewart Macaulay's classic study,[49] a business person—a purchasing agent—explains the reason:

> *If something comes up, you get the other man on the telephone and deal with the problem. You don't read legalistic contract clauses at each other if you*

University of St. Gallen, available at http://www.knowledge-communication.org/pdf/complextoclearnew.pdf. See also Eppler, M.J. and Burkhard, R.A. (2004) *Knowledge Visualization. Towards a New Discipline and its Fields of Application.* ICA Working Paper #2/2004, University of Lugano, available at http://www.bul.unisi.ch/cerca/bul/pubblicazioni/com/pdf/wpca0402.pdf.
48   Wordle is a free application for generating "word clouds" from text that you provide, available at http://www.wordle.net.
49   Macaulay, S. (1963) Non-contractual relations in business: a preliminary study. *American Sociological Review*, 28, 55–67, p. 61.

ever want to do business again. One doesn't run to lawyers if he wants to stay in business because one must behave decently.

The problem does not necessarily lie with lawyers, though. Many business, project and risk managers have overlooked the importance of their involvement in the contracting process and are pleased when lawyers drive contract design, drafting and negotiation. There is no shortage of reasons for this. The outcome is that contract design and drafting have become lawyer-dominated phases where the *real deal* is translated into a *paper deal* and, at worst, into legalese. In the process, many key decisions have been left to the lawyers, even in areas where business managers and subject matter experts could (and should) have made an important contribution. As stated by Deepak Malhotra, a Harvard Business School Professor, the latter are in a much stronger position to negotiate better outcomes and relationships, not just safer ones.[50]

In fact, once a contract has been drafted and signed, it often must be translated into ordinary language that ordinary people can understand. Why? Contracts are made for business performance purposes. To activate and guide that performance, the teams responsible for implementation need to truly understand the contract.

Research into companies' contract design capabilities confirms that the input of managers and engineers is needed in key areas to lay the foundation for the deal and construct

---

50   See, generally, Malhotra, D. (2012) Great deal, terrible contract: the case for negotiator involvement in the contracting phase. In B.M. Goldman and D.L. Shapiro (Eds.), *The Psychology of Negotiations in the 21st Century Workplace. New Challenges and New Solutions.* New York, NY: Routledge, pp. 363–98, 363–4.

operationally efficient contracts.[51] In earlier chapters we proposed a shift in the way contracts are viewed from legal rules to business management tools. This shift opens an array of new opportunities. Contracts are no longer separated from business and entrusted to the experts in an attempt to shift all risk to the other party. Instead, they become an integral part of business, used as tools that help the parties work together to reach clarity and make better decisions faster, with better results. As illustrated in Figure 6.8, the end result, ideally, is to enable the parties to achieve success through an ease of doing business that allows them to recognize, respond to, and manage risks together.

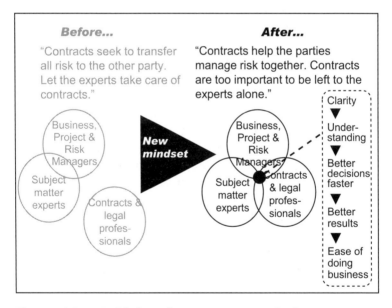

Figure 6.8   Bridging the gap: a new mindset

---

51   Argyres, N. and Mayer, K.J. (2007) Contract design as a firm capability: an integration of learning and transaction cost perspectives. *Academy of Management Review*, 32(4), October, 1060–77.

THE LEAN AND VISUAL (IKEA) APPROACH TO CONTRACT RISK MANAGEMENT

In Chapter 2, we viewed contracts as *visible scripts*—blueprints, roadmaps or sets of instructions—for collaboration. Contracts are similar to *user instructions*. Some instructions that accompany a piece of ready-to-assemble furniture, for example, can be difficult for users to follow. If only text is used, how many of the users would, for instance, know how to correctly select the different screw head types that are needed?

Compare the instructions of IKEA, which include images and diagrams of screws and how they connect with the furniture panels, along with showing the steps of assembly.[52] IKEA instructions use many images, and as few words as possible, to illustrate the required actions. This is supported by an intuitive design that tries to make it obvious how the pieces should be put together. The goal is to make the task of self-assembly foolproof, so that anyone can construct the furniture correctly just by following simple instructions and using a few basic tools. How different this is from most contracts, contract briefs, or process descriptions, including those that explain how to implement contracts or manage risk. These tend to use words only, with few or no images. Because their underlying design is seldom intuitive, the user must refer to the documents to find out what to do and not to do. The tools are not easy to use and often require special expertise. Since

---

52   See, for example, assembly instructions for an IKEA chair, available at http://www.ikea.com/ms/en_US/customer_service/assembly/B/B30093154.pdf, and for an IKEA shelf, available at http://www.ikea.com/ms/en_US/customer_service/assembly/F/F90086985.pdf.

the process is not foolproof, people make simple mistakes that could be easily avoided.[53]

A professional mechanic or carpenter might cope with word-only instructions, likely written by professionals for use by other professionals—as most contracts are written by lawyers essentially for use by other lawyers. This raises the question of whether the authors of words-only instructions want average users to be able to use them, or instead want to force users to hire trained members of an assemblers' guild. There are often too many rules and too much bureaucracy in contracting processes and documents for any busy business person to master. These rules can present a barrier to generating new business and cause weaknesses in implementation, easily leading to lost revenue, missed opportunities, and dissatisfied customers. While their goal is to mitigate risk, traditional instructions may in fact become sources of risk.

David Hillson, known as the Risk Doctor, has suggested a fresh, simplified approach to risk, calling it the IKEA approach. According to him, managing risk would be much easier if we adopted the IKEA approach to documenting the risk process. This means that we should:[54]

- Provide a checklist of what is needed at the start, and clearly describe the intended outcome

---

53   The IKEA examples here are adapted from Hillson, D. (2011) The IKEA approach to risk. *Project Manager Today*, June, 15, available at http://www.risk-doctor.com/docs/RiskDoctor0811-15.pdf, and Barton, T.D., Berger-Walliser, G. and Haapio H. (2011) Visualization: seeing contracts for what they are, and what they could become. In R.F. Henschel (Ed.), *Proceedings of the 2011 IACCM Academic Symposium for Contract and Commercial Management, Tempe (AZ), USA, 26 October 2011.* Ridgefield, CT: The International Association for Contract and Commercial Management, pp. 3–15.
54   Hillson 2011.

- Use a minimum number of words, with diagrams illustrating the most important parts of the process

- Ensure that all instructions can be understood by a normal person, with no specialist jargon or technical language

- Design the process logically so that it is obvious what to do next

- Provide all the required tools and make sure they do exactly what is needed

- Use high-quality components that have been well tested and proven to work

- Check that nothing essential has been left out before we release the process.

Managing contracts and contract risks could be much easier and more effective if we adopted a lean and visual (IKEA) approach to documenting them and the management process, using fewer words, more visualizations, and simpler tools. Well-designed, user-friendly contracts and processes can make it much easier for the parties to succeed together. The goal should be a list of simple steps in a logical order, with less words and more images, supported by tools that work and are easy to use.

SUMMARY

This chapter has discussed ways to recognize, review, and respond to contract risks. The chapter illustrates that in many cases, skills and resources that already exist need to be coordinated. While common tools and systematic processes can help, too much bureaucracy should be avoided. To succeed in managing contract risks and opportunities and benefit from this chapter, you should:

1. Make sure your contracting processes and risks, along with response plans, have an owner and that you have a plan in place to support systematic risk and opportunity management. Use your Contract Risk and Opportunity Management Plan throughout the contract lifecycle and especially where you need to secure a successful handoff to a new team.

2. Develop user-friendly processes and tools that help identify possible risks and ways to mitigate those risks when the contract is negotiated and throughout its performance. Share those tools with your contract partners and work together to develop and implement effective risk management.

3. Be prepared to share risks rather than attempting to allocate all risks to the other party. Risk allocation may mislead your organization into believing that its risk exposure has been minimized.

4. Make sure that responsibility for managing each risk is clearly allocated to the party best able to manage it and that the party is aware of this responsibility. Understand the difference between *risk allocation* and *risk management*. There is much more to true contract risk management than risk allocation and risk transfer.

5. Tackle the causes of risk, reduce their probability and impact, and focus on high-priority issues. Remember that

the strategies used for the recognition and management of risk are also suitable for the recognition and management of opportunities.

6. Simplify where you can. Make your goal user-friendly contracts and contract risk management tools that help project and delivery teams implement contracts and manage the risks.

7. Engage and empower your organization to make informed decisions. Use visual tools to communicate contracts and risks effectively. Adopt a lean and visual (IKEA) approach to contract risk management.

(7) Conclusion

Whenever businesses collaborate, buy, or sell, contracts are present. So are contract risks. Some contract risks are recognized and accepted, eyes wide open, as legitimate trade-offs. Others may remain unrecognized. Unrecognized risks lead to unmanaged risks.

The ultimate goal of contracts, as seen in this book, is *reaching business objectives*. To remain in business and reach objectives, one must make contracts and take risks. Ideally, the risks are taken *knowingly*. Yet there are various uncertainties about reaching objectives in business deals and relationships. Contract risk management is about managing those uncertainties.

Contract risks may be caused, for example, by expectations, requirements, or responsibilities that are not identified and fulfilled, leading to disappointments, disputes, liabilities, and remedies. Or they may be caused by unfavorable contract terms that could have been avoided or mitigated. Contrary to what some people think, successful management of contract risk is not just about contract clauses that address risk and the consequences of failure. Nor is successful contract risk management solely concerned with risk allocation or attempts to transfer all risks to the other party of the contract. The big picture requires a more holistic view. Increasingly, business leaders recognize that contracts are also about enabling sound risk taking, balancing risk with reward, sharing risks and managing them together, and developing and maximizing opportunities.

To achieve success with this holistic perspective you should:

1. Take a proactive approach to contracts—viewing them as business enablers and managerial tools rather than only legal tools. Remember that the right contract structure and terms can make all the difference between success and failure, profit and loss, and customer/supplier satisfaction and dissatisfaction.

2. Become contractually literate, because contract literacy is the foundation for identifying and managing contract risks and opportunities. It involves understanding not only what the contract says but also what it does *not* say and what that means.

3. Be aware of the risks related to unlimited liability, whether created through visible (express) or invisible (implied) terms. Do not accept such liability or expect your contract partners to do so without appropriate balance with a reward.

4. Instead of emphasizing the consequences of failure and contract clauses dealing with them—like damages for breach of contract—focus on eliminating or minimizing the causes and likelihood of failure. This focus begins with a shared understanding of contract requirements, change management, and other IACCM Top Terms of the Future.

5. Use an interest-based negotiation strategy that, instead of asking counterparties what they want, focuses on why they want it. Make sure that your negotiation team's mindset focuses on implementation rather than deal making alone. Adopt *lean contracting* practices that enable you to focus on your business goals.

6. Use your contracting processes and documents proactively as planning and decision making tools to safeguard that risks are taken *knowingly*, balanced with reward, and managed. Do not let gaps in the contracting process, poor communication, or lack of contract management lead to unmanaged risks or opportunities. Make sure that your contracting processes and risks, along with response plans, have an owner.

7. Understand the difference between *risk allocation* and *risk management*. Remember that allocating or transferring the risk to the other side does not make the risk disappear. Both sides need to recognize and respond to risks.

8. Do not accept anything you do not fully understand. Even boilerplate provisions and small print can have a big impact.

9. Develop user-friendly processes and tools that help secure success by identifying possible risks and ways to mitigate them. Share those tools with your contract partners and work together to develop and implement effective risk management.

10. Be prepared to share risks rather than attempting to allocate all risks to the other party. Make sure that responsibility for managing each risk is clearly allocated to the party

best able to manage it and that the party is aware of this responsibility.

11. Use new tools, including *lean contracting, contract visualization,* and a *lean and visual (IKEA) approach,* to increase interest, engage people, and communicate contracts and risks effectively. Make contract risk management and implementation easy, even for your contract partners.

12. Set up a managerial–legal team to introduce a new mindset that no longer sees contracts as just legal tools, focusing on worst case scenarios. Provide tools and training that guide your organization toward contract literacy so it is empowered to make informed decisions and manage contract risks and opportunities on an ongoing basis.

This book provides details for implementing these recommendations, as well as many additional action items. It also provides extracts and samples of contract risk lists, review checklists, matrices, and other tools that you can use as part of your Contract Risk and Opportunity Management Plan. We hope that individually or in combination, they will enable you and your organization to create value and achieve sustainable success.

Index

If you have found this book useful you may be interested in other titles from Gower

A Short Guide to Risk Appetite
Nick Obolensky
Paperback: 978-1-4094-4094-9
e-book: 978-1-4094-4095-6

A Short Guide to Customs Risk
Catherine Truel
Paperback: 978-1-4094-0452-1
e-book: 978-1-4094-0453-8

A Short Guide to Equality Risk:
Tony Morden
Paperback: 978-1-4094-0450-7
e-book: 978-1-4094-0451-4

Visit **www.gowerpublishing.com** and

- search the entire catalogue of Gower books in print
- order titles online at 10% discount
- take advantage of special offers
- sign up for our monthly e-mail update service
- download free sample chapters from all recent titles
- download or order our catalogue